CW00419640

THE FATHER OF THE BRONTËS

THE AUTHOR W W YATES *(Courtesy Dewsbury Reporter)*

THE FATHER OF THE BRONTËS

W W YATES

IMELDA MARSDEN
2006

First Printed in 1897
This facsimile reprint 2006
by Imelda Marsden
18 Quarryfields
Mirfield, WF14 0NT

ISBN 0 9552695 0 4

Printed and bound by
Smith Settle Printing and Bookbinding Ltd
Ilkley Road, Otley, West Yorkshire LS21 3JP

SPONSORS

Without the support of the following this publication would not have been possible

---

John Barber, Crossley Farm, Mirfield; Barclays Bank, Mirfield (Bryn Sutcliffe); The Beauty Works, Mirfield; Binks Vertical; Cherie Blair, Downing St, London; Pam Brindle; Brontë Society; Castles Carpets, Mirfield; Chadwick & Lawrence Solicitors, Dewsbury; Cloggs Coffee Shop, Mirfield; Cowley family; Mrs Crowther, Clough House, Hightown; Damons Hairdressers; Dewsbury Chamber of Trade; Bernard Diskin; Diskin & Co Solicitors, Dewsbury; Bob Duckett; Landlord, Dusty Miller, Mirfield; Mabel & John Ferrett; Foxes Biscuits; Kevin Fisher MBE; Gales Milliners, Dewsbury; Dudley Green; Prof Sellchi Hahinoto, Japan; Malcolm Haigh; Mary Haigh, America; Haigh's Farm Shop, Mirfield; Audrey Hall; Dr Graham Hardy; Norah & Tom Harrington; Healds Hall, Liversedge; Hatchard & Daughters Bookshop, Haworth; Gill Hawksworth; Linda & Michael Hutchinson; Inghams, Healds House, Dewsbury; Jacksons Shoe Shop, Mirfield; Kalon, Birstall; Ann Law; Leeds Golf Centre; Ann Lennon, Ireland; Margaret Livingstone, Ireland; David & Catherine Marsden; Margaret McCarthy; Maureen McMahon, Ireland, Tom Megahy; D&M Middleton; Rawfolds Mill, Cleckheaton; Mirfield Fire Station; Mirfield Historical Society; Mirfield Round Table; Mirfield Town Council; The Old Colonial, Mirfield; Joan Pinder; Rohn & Hassal UK, Dewsbury; Neil & Margaret Saville; Geoffrey & Heather Sharpe; Kevin Sheridan; Christine Silverwood; Darren Smith Builders Ltd; Soroptismist International of Dewsbury; Brian Speak; Spen Valley Civic Society; Frances Stott; Techsen Engineering, Dewsbury; Carl & William Thomas, America; Jean Todd; Toll House Book Shop, Holmfirth; Mandy Tyas; Wasp Nest, Mirfield; Wellhouse Moravian Church, Mirfield; Wellhouse Playschool, Mirfield; Westfield Nurseries, Mirfield; Mr & Mrs White, New Charnwood, Heckmondwike; Dr P Wintersgill; Yorkshire Bank, Mirfield; Deborah Youlton.

FOREWORD

William Walsh Yates was the author of *The Father of the Brontës* published in 1897, and was one of the founder members of the Brontë Society in 1893, a member of the Brontë Society Council and at one time its Chairman. He was brought up in Warrington, Lancashire. In the early days he worked as a commercial traveller and in his prime he enlisted in the 29th West Yorkshire Rifle Volunteers and was a Company colour sergeant. He came to West Yorkshire and lived there for nearly 60 years. He was editor of the *Dewsbury Reporter* newspaper, and became the oldest working journalist in Yorkshire, holding an honoured place in the ranks of journalism and wielding great influence with his pen.

William Yates left an indelible mark upon Dewsbury by being involved in the development of the town and public institutions. He was on the board of Dewsbury District Infirmary and at one time its President. Education meant a great deal to him and he was one of the promoters of Dewsbury Technical School. In ways too varied to mention he devoted much energy to promoting philanthropic and public works for the good of the town. For a numbers of years he was an Independent Dewsbury town councillor.

Mr Yates was keenly interested in the remarkable Brontë family and was the prime originator in setting up the Brontë Society. Sadly he did not live to see the Brontë museum move to the Brontë Parsonage in 1928 from a room above the Yorkshire Penny Bank in Main Street, Haworth. He died on

Monday 29th April 1918 aged 88 leaving a son and two daughters. His wife had died several years earlier after they had celebrated their golden wedding anniversary.

Mr Yates presented many papers and wrote articles on various matters relating to the Brontë family. His work in this direction included a life of the Reverend Patrick Brontë. He read the first paper to the inaugural Brontë Society AGM in December 1894 at Dewsbury Town Hall. His talk was about the Brontë family in the Dewsbury district whilst another founder member, Dr Erskine Stuart, gave an informative talk.

In 1893 Mr Yates had the idea of starting a Brontë Society and museum and approached Alderman Sir John Briggs of Keighley having been given a letter of introduction from a Dewsbury man. Sir John Briggs invited him to meet a few friends at the Liberal Club in Bank Street, Bradford to discuss plans. This led to a public meeting, in response to a circular issued by Mr Yates and another founder member Mr Joseph Horsfall Turner, schoolmaster, writer and antiquarian. The meeting was called by the Mayor of Bradford in the Council Chamber at Bradford Town Hall on 16th December 1893 attended by over 60 people. Mr Yates proposed the Brontë Society be formed and a museum established to display drawings, manuscripts, paintings, personal relics, editions of the works of the Brontë sisters and books relating to them. These suggestions were adopted and so the Brontë Society was formed and a date set for a committee to be formed.

The first meeting of the Brontë Society was held at the Free Library, Bradford on 13th January 1894 and the President and Council members elected. The President was Lord Houghton, Marquis of Crewe; the Vice-Presidents were Sir Wemyss Reid; Mr Augustine Birell Esq; Mrs Dormestier; George Smith, publisher; His Grace the Duke of Devonshire; Mr H I Butterfield Esq; Sir Isaac Holden Bart MP, Rev Robert Collyer DD, New York; Mr C Milnes Gaskell Esq; Rev William Wright DD; and Dr Peter Boyne.

The Brontë Society Council had 18 members including the Chairman Alderman Sir John Briggs JP; Mr F C Galloway, Treasurer; Mr Butler Wood, Bibliographical Secretary; and Mr Joseph Horsfall Turner, Corresponding Secretary. *Brontë Society Transactions* were published from 1895. The museum in the room above the Yorkshire Penny Bank, Main Street, Haworth began to be very overcrowded so other premises were sought for the museum. Oakwell Hall, Birstall was for sale and considered but the Brontë Parsonage came up for sale. Mr Roberts bought the parsonage and gave it to the Brontë Society for use as a museum in 1928.

I first read *The Father of the Brontës* by Mr W W Yates when I was fourteen years old and have read it several times since, before eventually owning a copy of the book. I was giving a talk about Patrick Brontë and about the book and a lady at the talk suggested that it should be reprinted.

Rev. Patrick Brontë made his mark in Dewsbury and Hartshead and certainly was a man before his time. The book has a chapter on Currer Bell in Mirfield and Dewsbury. This was one of the books written in the 1890's by one of the founder members of the Brontë Society. It is worth being put back on the bookselves to be read again.

Imelda Marsden 2005
Life member of the Bronte Society

INTRODUCTION

It would be difficult to exaggerate the significance of the writings of the various members of the Brontë family both with regard to English literature as a whole and more specifically in relation to the West Riding of Yorkshire within which all that creative activity happened. Enthusiasm for the work of Anne, Charlotte and Emily Brontë shows no signs of waning and indeed some most significant work has been produced in the past twenty years. Perhaps the most notable contribution to Brontë study has been Dr Juliet Barker's magnificent reassessment of the biographical background of the whole family; Juliet herself writes from within the context of West Yorkshire.

Fascinatingly enough William Walsh Yates' 1897 publication *The Father of the Brontës* heralds some developments that have really only been worked out in their fullness in these past two decades. There has been a long history of vilification of Patrick Brontë and a great misunderstanding of both his personality and his contribution both to the Brontë family and also to the wider community during his time as a priest in the West Riding. Yates' book already goes someway to correcting this view. Implicitly there is some criticism of Mrs Gaskell's famous biography of Charlotte Brontë. He notes at one point in his book '... an injustice has thereby been done to this memory (the memory of Patrick Brontë) by Charlotte Brontë's great biographer Mrs Gaskell.' Part of this injustice was underestimating the 'warm hearted generosity towards poor relations', amongst other things that was part of the Brontë father's personality and character.

This suggests that Patrick Brontë was austere but nevertheless well liked. It is clear from Yates account that Brontë was no rollicking character or an enthusiast; there was a profound seriousness to him and he was in many ways fairly reserved. Nevertheless alongside this there was a warmth to his personality and he was keen to right injustices where he could. There is a particularly fascinating account of the way in which he worked with Lord Palmerston, one of the great personalities of the age, in trying to defend someone who had been unjustly accused. Palmerston had been a fellow undergraduate at Cambridge with Patrick Brontë.

Elsewhere Yates points to Brontë's care for individuals. He also suggests that 'story-telling' was a hereditary gift in the Brontë family, Patrick himself having inherited it from his father. Fairly late on in his book Yates points out how 'the girls would hang on their father's lips as he depicted scene after scene of some tragic story in glowing words and with harrowing details'. This would go some way to explaining how three young women brought up in the sheltered background of an austere Yorkshire parsonage could produce the melodramatic novels that were shocking to many people within mid-Victorian society. Indeed it was this very issue that provoked Mrs Gaskell to produce a biography that painted Patrick Brontë in the rather harsh light in which he later came to be seen for more than one hundred and fifty years.

Yates' book is a fascinating insight into the heredity literary talent of the Brontë family and it also has some intriguing light to throw on the history of West Yorkshire. His descriptions of the vicarage at Dewsbury and of Roehead School, where Charlotte was both a pupil and then a teacher, are of interest to both Brontë enthusiasts and local Yorkshire people alike. This is also true of the links that he outlines with St John's Dewsbury Moor, which Church Charlotte attended when she moved from Roehead to teach at Miss Wooler's new school at Dewsbury Moor.

It is commendable that energy and insight have come together to republish William Walsh Yates' book more than one century on. Hopefully it will stimulate more interest not only in the Brontës, but also in the landscape in which they themselves were formed. It may also, alongside the work of Juliet Barker and others, help redress the unbalanced picture that has dominated the scene for more than a century and a half following the death of Charlotte, her sisters and her father.

Stephen Platten *July 2005*
Bishop of Wakefield

THE FATHER OF THE BRONTËS

Facsimile

THE REVD. P. BRONTË, B.A., 1856.

THE FATHER OF THE BRONTËS

His Life and Work at Dewsbury and Hartshead

WITH A CHAPTER ON "CURRER BELL'

BY

W. W. YATES

(Fellow of the Institute of Journalists)

"THERE IS A HISTORY IN ALL MEN'S LIVES."

Leeds:

FRED. R. SPARK AND SON.

1897.

THIS BOOK IS DEDICATED

BY THE AUTHOR

TO THE PEOPLE OF DEWSBURY AND THE DISTRICT,

AMONGST WHOM HE HAS LIVED AND WORKED

FOR MORE THAN THIRTY-SIX YEARS,

AND FOR WHOSE STERLING QUALITIES OF HEART AND MIND

HE HAS GREAT ADMIRATION.

PREFACE.

In the following comparatively few chapters will be found the fruit of patient investigations, extending, with long intervals, from the year 1879, and it is hoped that the perusal will tend to enable the reader to form a clearer estimate of the man, Patrick Brontë, and remove misapprehensions. When the Revd. gentleman came to Dewsbury he was an entire stranger, and only the clergyman who engaged him to act as curate of the parish would know anything of his past career. Certain prominent traits of character, and incidents in which he played a not unimportant part, soon, however, brought him into notice. He resided here but a couple of years, his stay in Hartshead was of but little longer duration, and had it not been that he became the father of children who achieved fame in his lifetime, it is not at all likely that he would have had a place, however humble, in the literary annals of our country. Still, he was a man of considerable parts, of great strength of mind, undaunted courage, and true manliness, and it is well that those who worship his daughters as literary celebrities should know more than they have had the opportunity of learning about his character.

Having riper knowledge of the father, they may be all the more able to appreciate the genius of the daughters, and trace here and there in the writings at least of two of them the influence which has given that genius its wider knowledge of human nature and deeper insight into character.

To obtain reliable particulars of the life Mr. Brontë led whilst in this parish, of the people he met, and the scenes he passed through, has been a difficult task, and I can only claim that I have performed it conscientiously and to the best of my ability. Fortunately, I have had the cordial help of many friends, and I would especially acknowledge the services rendered by the Revd. J. R. Baldwin, Vicar of Dewsbury from 1879 to 1881, now of Ilfracombe, who placed the parish registers at my disposal for local historical investigation; by his successor, the Revd. Canon Whitby, of Sandown, Isle of Wight; by the present Vicar, the Revd. Canon Lowther Clarke, for similar valuable privileges; and by the Revd. Thos. King, Vicar of Hartshead, who permitted searches of the register books of that parish some years ago, and sent me interesting items of information. To Mr. Clement K. Shorter and

To Dr. Robertson Nicoll, of London, I am also greatly indebted. But others have been most kind, among them Mr. J. J. Stead, of Heckmondwike, who not only gave me useful photographs from his large collection, but came over to Dewsbury and took others of considerable interest; Mr. Frank Peel, of the same Town; Mr. W. S. Cameron, F.J.I., of Leeds; Mr. C. A. Craven, of Savile Town, Dewsbury; Mrs. A. Sheard and Mrs. Abm. Hirst, of Roberttown, Liversedge; the Misses Smith, of Dewsbury Moor; Mrs. Walliss, Mrs. M. Rhodes, and Messrs. Ward and Co., of Dewsbury. Lastly, I name my daughter, Miss Yates, who has been indefatigable and most painstaking in assisting me to unravel the oft-tangled web of local story. Others who have kindly given their help are named elsewhere, and to all I beg to tender my grateful thanks.

With these acknowledgments I present "THE FATHER OF THE BRONTËS" to the Subscribers and the Public, in the hope that its perusal will lead to a knowledge of the real character of a man who has been much misrepresented because he was not understood.

W. W. Y.

Dewsbury, *August, 1897.*

CONTENTS.

CHAPTER I.

CHAPTER II.

CHAPTER III.

CHAPTER IV.

CHAPTER V.

CHAPTER VI.

CHAPTER VII.

CHAPTER VIII.

CHAPTER IX.

CHAPTER X.

CHAPTER XI.

CHAPTER XII.

CHAPTER XIII.

CHAPTER XIV.

CHAPTER XV.

CHAPTER XVI.

CHAPTER XVII.

CHAPTER XVIII.

CHAPTER XIX.

OUR ILLUSTRATIONS.

A few words about the illustrations scattered through the pages of the work will prove of interest.

The portrait of Mr. Brontë, as a young man, is from a painting which Mr. Clement K. Shorter, in *The Sketch* of the 21st of April last, states the revd. gentleman sat for whilst at Wellington, in order to make it a present to his friend, the Revd. John Nunn, curate of Shrewsbury, afterwards rector of Thorndon, Suffolk. Miss M. Lipton, a niece of Mr. Nunn, has possession of the original, and has kindly allowed it to be copied.

The second likeness of Mr. Brontë, depicting him as an old man, is from a photograph by Mr. J. J. Stead, and taken from a glass "positive:" *temp.* about 1856.

The third portrait is that of Miss Maria Branwell (afterwards Mrs. Brontë) at the age of fifteen. It is a reproduction obtained through the kindness of Mr. Shorter, of a photograph of one of a set of likenesses of the Branwell family—father, mother, and two daughters—and published by him, with others, in *The Sketch.*

Another picture is by Mr. Stead, a photograph of a miniature of the Revd. Hammond Roberson, vicar of Liversedge, and formerly curate at Dewsbury. The painting was by a first-class artist, and has been pronounced by Mr. Henry Roberson, nephew of the deceased (formerly of Healds House, Dewsbury Moor, and afterwards of Reepham, Norfolk, where he died at the age of 94 years) to be an admirable likeness.

A *fac-simile* of a letter by the Revd. Hammond Roberson is also furnished, and, as will be seen, it has some local interest. He was a man of much force of character, who made his mark in the district in many ways, and assisted to establish in 1783 what is claimed to be the oldest Sunday School north of the Trent—that connected with Dewsbury Parish Church.

A copy of a page of the register of marriages in use when Mr. Brontë was curate at Dewsbury is also given, photographed specially for this work by Mr. Stead. In no instance, in all the pages of the volume covering the time the revd. gentleman was at the church, is the accent in the name Brontë marked as in the Haworth registers, and now universally by all writers, by the diæresis, a simple tick being made to suffice, as in the four signatures in the page. The exact shape varies, but all Mr. Brontë aimed at was evidently to show that the pronunciation of the name was "Bronty."

Amongst other illustrations is one showing Dewsbury Church as it existed about 1837. There is none, we believe, of earlier date in the century. During the last seventeen years or so the fabric has undergone considerable alteration and enlargement; and of the church as it existed in Mr. Brontë's days, there only remains the north aisle (a typical specimen of what is known as churchwardens' Gothic) and the tower. Mention is made in subsequent chapters of a "three-decker" pulpit from which Mr. Brontë and other clergymen preached. It was demolished long ago, as were the old-fashioned high-backed pews that occupied the floor of the church. The north and south galleries, and what was known as the singing loft have also disappeared. In the view we give the vicarage is shown, but only very inadequately.

A copy of a photograph specially taken by Mr. Stead, showing the fireplace in the drawing-room of the old vicarage, will have an interest for many members of the Dewsbury parish congregation, and particularly to those of them who were connected with the Church Institute, which for many years found a lodgment in the ancient dwelling. Flanking the fireplace (and necessarily included in the view) are two Gothic doorways from the Old Church. The oaken door in one arch yet remains, and the date of its construction and placing within the stonework, is seen in the iron studs it bears. These had to be temporarily whitened to secure them being seen in the photograph, a device that even the most devoted of antiquaries will perhaps forgive. These, with a view to their preservation, are built against the north wall of the churchyard, and stand some twenty yards from a much more ancient and interesting relic of antiquity, the Old Moot Hall, which dates from feudal times.

We also present a *fac-simile* of Charlotte Brontë's handwriting, with signature, in a photograph taken for us many years ago. It is a copy of one page of a letter addressed by her to a friend, and was lent to us by the late Mr. Matthew Ridgway, J.P., of Dewsbury. He had obtained it and other autographs from Dr. Henry Hemingway, but how it came into possession of that gentleman is not known. The interesting relic belongs to Mr. Alfred Ridgway, a son of the first-named gentleman. To whom it was addressed, none of the three knew, but a few weeks ago, a copy having been shown to Charlotte's life-long friend, Miss Ellen Nussey, she expressed the belief that it was written to Miss Leah Brooke, of Dewsbury, a daughter of Mr. John Brooke, of Aldams House, afterwards of Fall Lane, and that the Miss Mary referred to would be a sister of Miss Leah. The latter, for six months or so, was a school-fellow of Miss Nussey and of the shy maiden, who in a few short years became one of the most distinguished of English writers. Mr. Brooke, the father of Leah and Mary, was in his youth and early manhood an attorney's clerk, but showing great commercial ability, he was offered a place in the works of Mr. Halliley, at Aldams Mills. Subsequently he was taken into partnership, and the firm carried on business under the style of Halliley, Son, and Brooke, woollen manufacturers, merchants, and bankers. Among existing local curiosities are Dewsbury one-pound notes, issued by them.

After her father's death, Miss Mary Brooke alone or with a sister, took up the teaching profession, and conducted a school of high repute near Fall Lane, Dewsbury. She was a devoted churchwoman, and highly respected in the town and neighbourhood.

A view of Roehead, where Charlotte Brontë was both scholar and teacher, is also among our illustrations, and will interest the reader.

Does Miss Mary still retain her situation—
is she well and happy?
I would write a longer letter to you but
it is getting so very late—and I am sleepy
Remember me respectfully to your mother
and kindly to your sisters and believe
me my dear Miss Leah
Yours half-asleep but very sincerely
C Brontë

FAC-SIMILE OF A LETTER BY "CURRER BELL" TO A DEWSBURY LADY.

CHAPTER I.

INTRODUCTORY—THE ANCIENT PARISH OF DEWSBURY—PAULINUS—DOMESDAY BOOK—CONSTITUTION OF A VICARAGE—THE CHURCH REGISTERS, ANCIENT AND MODERN—MR. BRONTË AND HIS CURACIES.

As copies of this work may find their way into the hands of readers unacquainted with the parish of Dewsbury, where in the township of that name, and in Hartshead, the Revd. Patrick Brontë laboured between five and six years, it will not be deemed out of place if, before beginning the story of his life and work therein, we furnish some account of the parish, which has an interesting ecclesiastical history, dating from remote times, as will be seen.

The first mention of Dewsbury is in Domesday Book, where, treating of what would be rather less than the present township, it is recorded—

"In Dewsberia there are three carucates to be taxed, which two ploughs will till. This land belongs to Wakefield, yet King Edward had it in a manor. It now belongs to the King, and there are six villaues and two bordars, with four ploughs, a priest and a church. The whole manor is four quarentens long and the same broad. In the time of King Edward the value was ten shillings; it is the same now."

But tradition, for which there is not a little warrant, takes us back to a more remote period, namely to A.D. 627, when Paulinus, the Roman missionary, preached and baptised here, about thirty years after the landing of St. Augustine on our shores. Some antiquaries, among them Mr. S. J. Chadwick, F.S.A., of Dewsbury, are of opinion that when Paulinus came he found a cross already set up, somewhere about the site of the present church of Dewsbury. For purposes of baptism, conducted as it was in those early days, the position was well selected, as the river Calder was near, and so was a wide running brook, and, as the subsoil shows, the land was free from bog. On this supposed site, well chosen for his active labours of conversion, portions of "runic" crosses have been found; erected they must have been at a period long anterior to the days of King Edward the Confessor, dating back, in fact, to early Saxon times. All these relics are carefully preserved, and may be seen at any time by visitors to Dewsbury Church. One is described as showing in the carving on the reverse of the centre or boss of what has been a cross—probably placed over a grave—a reference to sun worship, and on the obverse to Christianity; the inference being that the deceased was one of those converted from heathenism.

Interesting speculations arise, but they cannot be pursued in these pages. It may however be named that at Whalley, on the Lancashire Calder—to which the old parish of Dewsbury extended—there are several "runic" crosses like the relic above mentioned. Reference is made to them by that learned antiquary, Dr. Whitaker, in his *History of Whalley*.

Dewsbury was an important religious centre long before the Norman Invasion, and from the river at Whalley and the district, the parish extended to and beyond our Yorkshire Calder, and covered an area of about four hundred square miles. Within this ecclesiastical domain—if the term be permitted—were several important parishes, among them Halifax—which paid an annual pension to the rectory of Dewsbury—Huddersfield, Bradford, Almondbury, Kirkheaton, Kirkburton, and Thornhill. The tribute by Halifax ceased long ago, but the rest still make a yearly payment to the vicar of Dewsbury.

The present parish consists but of the townships of Dewsbury, Ossett, Soothill, and Hartshead, the latter being separated from the mother place by the township of Mirfield, which obtained ecclesiastical independence through the efforts of Sir John Heton, in 1261.

When the Normans conquered this country King William gave away many manors and other estates to his followers, and among the former was that of Dewsbury. In 1338 the rectory manor reverted to the crown, and eleven years afterwards—as will be seen in another chapter—the present advowson was constituted; but there is little known about it until the times of the Tudors, except who were the successive vicars.

It is interesting to know, especially as some of the information obtained about Mr. Brontë—*temp.* 1809-10-11—comes from the register books, that these of Dewsbury are amongst the oldest in the kingdom (the first volume being from 1535), and contain information bearing upon national, county, or parochial affairs—chiefly, of course, the latter. It was whilst searching one of the books relating to the first few years of the present century that the discovery was made of Mr. Brontë having been a curate here. Mrs. Gaskell and other writers, prior to our mention, had said he went from Weathersfield to Hartshead, whereas he came to Dewsbury; but it is only quite recently that Mr. Shorter, author of *Charlotte Brontë and Her Circle*, ascertained and published the fact that Mr. Brontë proceeded from

No. 1839 William Hardcastle Blacksmith & Bach^r and Alice Hey Spinst^r both of this Parish were
Married in this Church by Banns
this Twenty fourth Day of June in the Year One Thousand Eight Hundred
and Ten By me P. Brontë, Curate,
This Marriage was solemnized between Us { Willm Hardcastle — / Alice + Hey's Mark }
in the Presence of { Joshua Littlewood / Wm Clayton Friends Bradford }

No. 1840 Thomas Farnhill Labourer & Elizabeth Oates Wid^w both of this Parish were
Married in this Church by Banns
this Second Day of July in the Year One Thousand Eight Hundred
and Ten By me P. Brontë, Curate
This Marriage was solemnized between Us { Thomas + Farns Mark / Elizabeth + Oates Mark }
in the Presence of { William Auty / Thos Smith }

No. 1841 Daniel Crossier Cloth^r & Bach^r & Hannah Blackburn both of this Parish were
Married in this Church by Banns
this Second Day of July in the Year One Thousand Eight Hundred
and Ten By me P. Brontë, Curate
This Marriage was solemnized between Us { Daniel X Crossier's Mark / Hannah + Blackburn's Mark }
in the Presence of { Geo Walker / John Crowshay }

No. 1842 Joseph Cocker Cloth^r & Bach^r and Hannah Haigh both of this Parish were
Married in this Church by Banns
this Ninth Day of July in the Year One Thousand Eight Hundred
and Ten By me P. Brontë, Curate
This Marriage was solemnized between Us { Joseph Cocker / Hannah + Haigh's Mark }
in the Presence of { John Haley / John Hepkelston }

FAC-SIMILE OF A PAGE OF DEWSBURY PARISH CHURCH REGISTERS.

the Essex parish to Wellington, where he acted as curate for some months, having gone to the pleasant parish near the foot of the Wrekin, that he might have the company of a former chum of his at Cambridge University—the Revd. John Nunn.

CHAPTER II.

BIOGRAPHICAL—PATRICK BRONTË'S EARLY LIFE—HIS LITERARY TASTES—PUBLISHES A VOLUME OF POEMS—LATER DAYS—MARRIAGE—BIRTHS AND DEATHS OF HIS CHILDREN.

Who was the Revd. Patrick Brontë? We are assuming, in putting this question, that few knew where he came from, whereas, comparatively few are they who are not familiar with portions, at least, of his life-story; still, we think it best, though this volume treats of him almost solely in his connection with Dewsbury and Hartshead, to give a biographical sketch, if in the briefest form:

Mr. Brontë was born on St. Patrick's day (March 17th), 1777, at Emdale, in the parish of Drumgooland, County Down, Ireland, and was the son of Hugh Brontë, a small farmer. At fourteen he went to learn hand-loom weaving with a friend of the family, named Robert Donald, and remained a few years, during which time he read much, and had the sympathetic assistance of the Revd. Andrew Hardshaw, a Presbyterian minister—in pursuing his studies, for the young fellow was able and ambitious. Through the efforts of the same good man he was appointed as teacher in a humble school at Glascar

Hill, not very far from his home, where, says Dr. W. Wright in *The Brontës in Ireland*, his scholars were largely the children of farmers and workpeople.

Whilst there he tried the muse, and, states the authority named, wrote most of the pieces published in 1811 among his *Cottage Poems*, touching them up in England. Leaving Glascar Hill school—the doctor tells us because he had written some verses to, and kissed the rather mature daughter of a local farmer, and had been complained of in consequence—he was appointed to a better seminary at Drumballyroney, under the vicar, the Revd. Thos. Tighe, and there he taught and studied, and saved money. In three years he quitted the place, came over to England, and guided by Mr. Tighe's advice, went to Cambridge, and entered St. John's College, this being on the 1st of October, 1802. Three days afterwards he commenced residence. Mr. Brontë's university career was satisfactory. He won several exhibitions, took the B.A. degree, this on the 23rd of April, 1806, in which year he was ordained, and was appointed to the curacy at Weatherfield, Essex. This he left in January, 1809, to be curate at Wellington, and thence came to Dewsbury.

In July, 1811, Mr. Brontë was presented by his vicar, the Revd. John Buckworth, M.A., with the living of Hartshead-cum-Clifton. In the same year he published his first book, the title of which was

Cottage Poems, and in December, 1812, married Miss Maria Branwell, a native of Penzance, and settled at Hightown, Liversedge, where two children were born to them—Maria and Elizabeth, who only lived for eleven and ten years respectively.

In 1815 Mr. Brontë exchanged livings with the incumbent of Thornton, the Revd. Thos. Atkinson, M.A., a nephew of the Revd. Hammond Roberson, M.A. (a famous man in his day and generation), and who died on the 9th of August, 1841. Whilst in this parish his children who became famous were born, namely, Charlotte, 1816; Patrick Branwell, 1817; Emily Jane, 1818; and Anne, 1819. Mr. Brontë removed to Haworth in 1820, having been appointed vicar, and he died there on the 7th of June, 1861. In the meantime he had published other works, one being issued when he lived at Thornton.

Mrs. Brontë died on the 15th of September, 1821, and their children, as under, namely: Maria, 6th of May, 1825; Elizabeth, 15th of June, in the same year; Patrick Branwell, 24th of September, 1848; Emily Jane ("Ellis Bell"), on the 19th of December following; Anne ("Acton Bell"), 28th of May, 1849; and Charlotte ("Currer Bell"), who had married the Revd. Arthur Bell Nicholls, B.A., 31st of March, 1855. His own death occurred on the 7th of June, 1861, at the age of eighty-five.

CHAPTER III.

MR. BRONTË'S LIFE AND CHARACTER—WHAT CRITICS HAVE SAID —WAS HE ROLLICKING, AMOROUS, OR MOROSE?—WAS HE ENTHUSIASTIC?—BURNS AND BRONTË, A COMPARISON AND A CONTRAST—EPISTLE TO THE VICAR OF DEWSBURY.

It would be a serious, nay, an unpardonable omission were not some account given of Mr. Brontë's ordinary life and work whilst curate at Dewsbury, especially as very remarkable statements about both have been published. One writer has described him as, in 1811—Mr. Brontë being then thirty-four years of age—"a rollicking, handsome, inflammable young Irishman." Rollicking he certainly was not; in fact he was serious-minded, as his conduct and writings prove, and though he fell in love with a young lady, Miss Mary Burdar, whilst at Weathersfield, surely that was not remarkable, seeing that when he took up the curacy there—a curacy in which he had sole charge—he was twenty-nine years old. If falling in love had taken place say ten years earlier, and had there been other sweethearts in the meantime, there would have been proof of inflammability, though not of rollicking.

2

We may be reminded of the verse-writing mentioned by Dr. Wright in his book, *The Brontës in Ireland*, and told that the kiss the young schoolmaster is said to have given to a farmer's daughter affords sufficient to justify what has been asserted. Not so. We regard the story as one of the romances told to the author when making his investigations in the sister country. One thing is clear, viz., that when Mr. Brontë left, whether he had to quit Glascar Hill because of what is said to have occurred or not, he received prompt promotion and had the support of his friend, the Presbyterian minister, and of the vicar, Mr. Tighe, who had the control of the "larger academy." Such a name as academy is, in fact, inapplicable to the first school, and the young master was miserably paid. We repeat, he received substantial promotion in the appointment he got through the minister his friend, and which was given to him by another divine. Had Mr. Brontë's conduct been shady he would not have had the support of these divines in gaining a better position in life. If there was nothing improper in his conduct, as we believe, then the incident was too trivial to have been recollected, especially in such a gallant and "inflammable" country as Ireland is reputed to be.

Was there any love making by him in Dewsbury?

We have not been able to learn of anything of the kind, nor to find warrant for the assertion of another writer, that "Mr. Brontë had the happy knack of falling in love with every pretty face he met," and that "folk who knew him used to smile at his faculty for adoration, and thought it was of a piece with his enthusiastic character."

That the revd. gentleman was handsome may safely be accepted, for he was tall, well-formed, and of good presence, and, as a portrait of him published by Mr. Shorter (and which we reproduce) shows, had fine and almost classic features. The typical Irishman is always inflammable where love is concerned—we know that by song and story—but the subject of our volume was not a type of his countrymen in that respect. Like them he was brave, impetuous, daring, proud, and generous, a good friend, and a good enemy where there was wrong doing, and there the resemblance may be said to end.

Was Mr. Brontë of "enthusiastic" character? We doubt it. The revd. gentleman had a clear conception of what he believed to be his duty, and fulfilled such obligations as lay before him; still he was impetuous, apt, perhaps, to take offence where none was intended, and to fly off at a tangent, as it were, under supposed taunt or sneer, going suddenly to other work than that upon which he had been engaged. That, however, was not the conduct of an enthusiast, who would have followed his purpose to the end, despite difficulties placed in his way, and certainly not have allowed insult or ridicule to cause him to turn aside. Mr. Brontë was an altogether different man: prompt in an emergency we know, self-reliant and strong, and he gained the regard of those around him; but there was the defect of character mentioned, and no doubt in the course of his long life he bitterly regretted its existence. One bad reader of character declares him to have been morose, which he certainly was not. A man at once rollicking and morose would indeed be a study in human nature. Of enthusiasm, as ordinarily understood, there seems in Mr. Brontë to have been hardly a trace, and what there was showed itself in the performance of his clerical duties. It certainly is not perceivable in his published poems, for all negative the idea of inflammability of heart. Search his books and where are the amorous verses? Where a poem to his mistress's eye-brow even, and where the tributes to the charms of the many fair creatures with whom he is asserted to have had "the happy knack of falling in love?"

In all the poems Mr. Brontë wrote there is only one that deals with the subject of Love. It is entitled, "Lines addressed to a lady on her birthday," and will be found in *The Rural Minstrel*, published at Halifax in 1813 It is accepted as having been written to Miss Branwell, the young lady he espoused in December, 1812, and he evidently thought it good enough to include in the little volume he issued soon after their union.

Burns was "inflammable." That we all know, and the world is greatly the richer for it through the influence of his genius. Indications of the existence of the passion of love appear in almost everything he wrote respecting woman. In him passion oft' burnt fiercely, and as oft' was subdued, and love was expressed in tenderness of feeling that, as given in his poems, has moved us all. But where is there anything even distantly approaching that in Mr. Brontë's writings, if we may compare the little with the great?

The fact is, the two men were essentially different in character and disposition, as in their respective callings. We are not called upon to say which was the better man, and merely contrast the two because one is said to have had what was a strong feature in the character of the other.

That Mr. Brontë had warm affections is undoubted. Such are the possession of every man and woman with sound minds in sound bodies, and he was as capable of inspiring love as of loving, and in that respect was no different from his fellows. Coming, as he did, from the Emerald Isle, the Irishman of the novel (with one characteristic omitted) has been accepted by some as a model of what he was sure to be by birth and breeding, and an injustice has thereby been done to his memory, not the least of the wrong-doing being by Charlotte Brontë's great biographer, Mrs. Gaskell. One prominent feature in the Irish character he possessed—warm hearted generosity towards poor relations, as has been named by more than one writer—by Mr. Frank Peel and Dr. Wright amongst the number.

It would be interesting to learn something of the life Mr. Brontë led when curate at Wellington, but we fear there is little likelihood of any information of value being forthcoming; or of it being told how the vicar of Dewsbury came to engage a curate living in a remote parish in the southern portion of Shropshire. Mr. Buckworth, whilst his health was good, travelled a little, and went away from his cure occasionally, and it may be that in one of the tours he took, the two came together. But why indulge in idle speculations? That he left Dewsbury more than once in search of health whilst Mr. Brontë was with him is known, the curate being left in full charge. A strong friendship had formed between the two men and how strong the feeling was on the part of the younger may be seen in his first published volume, *Cottage Poems*, printed at Halifax in 1811. Amongst the poetry is an "EPISTLE TO THE REVD. J—— B—— (evidently John Buckworth) WHILST JOURNEYING FOR THE RECOVERY OF HIS HEALTH," most probably composed at Dewsbury. There are nine and twenty stanzas, and from them we select three, for they show to some extent the character of the man, and what feelings he entertained towards his vicar :

When warmed with zeal my rustic muse
Feels fluttering fain to tell her news,
And paint her simple lowly views
　　With all her art,
And though in genius but obtuse
May touch the heart.

Of palaces and courts of kings
She thinks but little, never sings,
But wildly strikes her uncouth wings
　　In some poor cot ;
Spreads o'er the poor her fostering wings,
And soothes their lot.

* * * *

To all my heart is kind and true,
But glows with ardent love for you,
Though absent still you rise in view,
　　And talk and smile,
Whilst heavenly themes for ever new,
Our cares beguile.

* * * *

Another sample of his verse, exhibiting the kindly interest he took in the lowly, is his "EPISTLE TO THE LABOURING POOR." From it we take this stanza:

A fond farewell, each cottage friend
To Jesu's love I would commend
Your souls and bodies to the end
  Of life's rough way,
Then (Death subdued), may you ascend
  To endless day.

Mr. Newsam in his *Poets of Yorkshire*, published in 1845—two years before Charlotte Brontë got her first and greatest work, *Jane Eyre*, issued—has a few words about her father, mentioning his books, *Cottage Poems*, and *The Rural Minstrel*. He describes Mr. Brontë's works as presenting "pious sentiments in a plain garb," and few readers will challenge the correctness of the critic's statement.

CHAPTER IV.

MR. BRONTË AT DEWSBURY VICARAGE—HIS HABITS THERE—DESCRIPTION OF THE RESIDENCE—RIVER STROLLS—THE CALDER, A PELLUCID STREAM—WHAT IS IT NOW?

When living at the Dewsbury Vicarage the revd. gentleman had every opportunity given to him for study, a room for his separate use being allotted for his modest collection of books, his desk, &c. It was a small apartment leading out of the entrance hall on the west side, and pannelled, as were some of the other rooms, in oak, that long before had become dark from age. In this place he took his meals not unfrequently, and lived plainly, oatmeal being his principal food. The members of the household sometimes rallied him about his fare, and urged the keeping of a better table, but he always declined. An exception was made on Sundays, however, for all dined and supped together, but even then there was not as much enjoyment as might have been had from the table, for all the meats were cold. Mr. and Mrs. Buckworth, as well as the Curate, had strict opinions about the proper observance of the Sabbath, and it was made a day of rest from secular work: a day, of course, of religious labour.

The building in which these people lived was razed to the ground in 1889; and the site it occupied, together with the "convenient garden" and the "enclosure," now form part of the parish churchyard; and of the structure nothing now remains, except the oak timbers, nearly all bought by Mr. John Wormald, of Denton Park, near Ilkley, formerly of Ravens Lodge, Dewsbury, and a relic or two—one mentioned below. The external walls, covered on the south side from ground to roof with luxuriant ivy, were perhaps not more than 250 or 300 years old. Those in the interior, however, belonged to a much earlier period, and except where "restoration" had taken place, were constructed of oak logs, with wattle and daub, the whole lined with wainscotting of the same wood. A modern addition, used for some years as the library of the Dewsbury Church Institute, had, of course, none of these characteristics.

When the vicarage was established in 1349, an appropriation having been made to "the Dean and College of the Free Chapel in the Palace at Westminster"—St. Stephen's—the erection of a dwelling for the successive clergymen holding the living was ordered in the deed, this being the minimum accommodation to be provided, viz.: "In one competent mansion-house, well built, consisting of one hall, two chambers at the least, a kitchen, a stable, a granary, and a house for cattle, and other necessary purposes of the said vicar;" "likewise a convenient garden and an enclosure as big as the neighbourhood will allow of." This deed was signed and sealed on the 20th of June in the year named, and, as stated at the foot of the document, "given at our Manor of Ripon." The "mansion-house" was to be erected at the expense of the Dean and Chapter, and would be in all probability the finest residence in the locality, as well as a good example of the domestic architecture of the period. Many vicars it sheltered in long succession, broken once when the occupant of the living was ejected in Parliamentarian times, and a Presbyterian minister installed. The unfortunate vicar died in great poverty at Dewsbury.

At the time the house was being pulled down the mode of construction was disclosed, and much interest was taken in this by townspeople, many of whom openly expressed their regret at the demolition. Local readers will perhaps be interested in a description of the interior of this, the oldest house existing in the whole parish up to the time of its demolition, and we therefore furnish a necessarily brief account:

The rooms, many in number, comprised an entrance hall, a drawing room leading therefrom, in which was a large fire-place with cosy ingle nook. The masonry of this has been preserved as a relic of the old vicarage by being built into the north wall of the churchyard, and is depicted in this work. There was also a dining room, with doorway leading into what was called the breakfast room, but some years before the demolition this was bricked up. Leading out of the hall was Mr. Brontë's "den," and which a generation ago was denominated the butler's pantry. There was also a spacious kitchen and a scullery, the latter sometimes known as the pump-room, for it contained a pump, and beneath it a well from which the townspeople of the immediate neighbourhood fetched water—"it was so good for tea-making!" Was it, indeed? The well was in immediate contiguity to the graveyard, which for more than five hundred years was the only place of sepulture for the parishes of Dewsbury, Ossett, and Soothill. Five hundred years! A thousand would be probably a more correct estimate of the number. Sanitary science was not understood in the good old days when the house-mothers fetched water from the vicarage well that their tea might be brewed so strong and clear. Could these good old days give up their secrets we might learn perhaps how many deaths had been caused by the specially brewed "cup that cheers but does not inebriate."

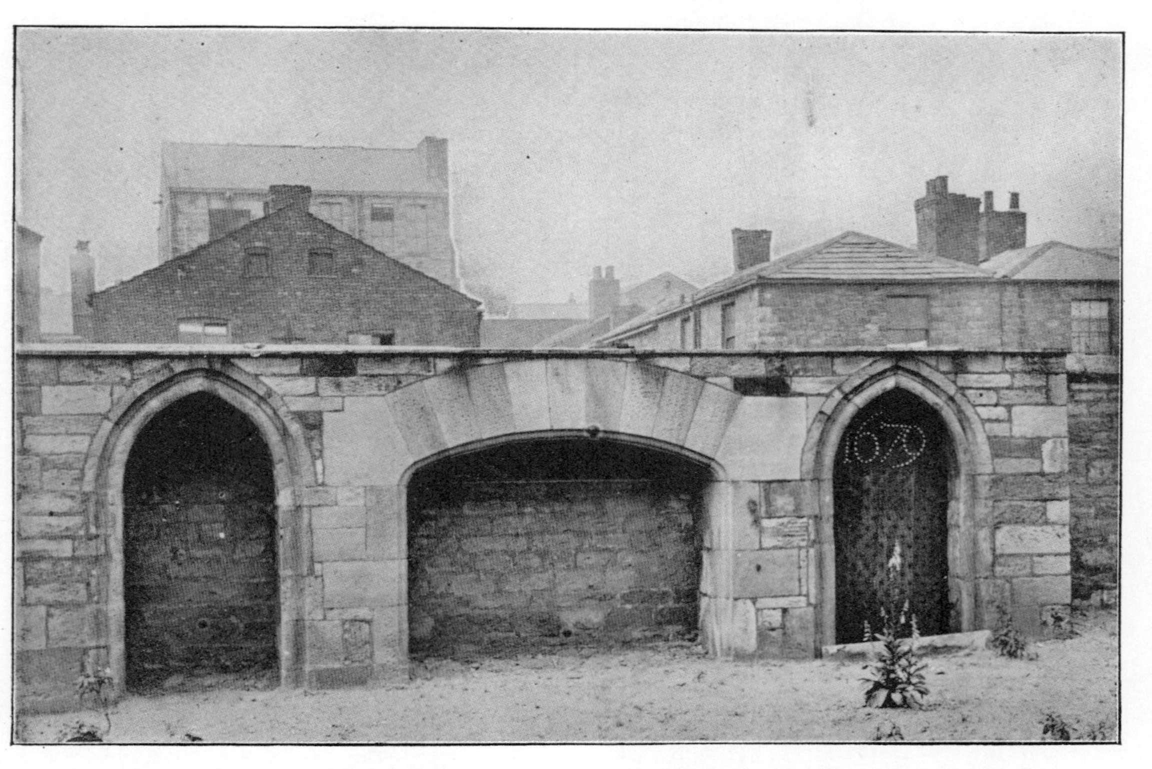

FIREPLACE FROM DEWSBURY VICARAGE, AND DOORWAYS FROM THE OLD PARISH CHURCH.

But the vicarage house still claims attention. There were two staircases, one being for the family and guests, the other for the servants. Ascending to the first story the visitor found several chambers, one with the reputation of being haunted by a lady in green! Another over the breakfast room was appropriated by Mr. Buckworth as a study, and in it he wrote sermons, and articles for magazines, and composed hymns, and some of the latter are popular to-day. One is that familiar in many nurseries and schools, commencing:

> "Great God, and wilt thou condescend,
> To be my Father and my Friend?"

Another has the title of "My Bible," and a third that of "The Sunday Scholar." Mr Buckworth issued hymns in book form, and he must have been actively engaged in this work when Mr. Brontë was with him. Mr. F. Inkersley, of Bradford, was the printer, and in the year after the curate had been presented with the living of Hartshead, Mr. Buckworth issued a fifth edition, this being in 1812. We have these particulars in a letter by Mr. S. J. Chadwick, sent to *Notes and Queries* some years ago. In a postscript he mentions that a twelfth edition, containing one hundred hymns, was published in 1844. Copies of these books are still in existence.

Mr. Brontë was fond of using the "convenient garden" attached to the vicarage, and also the "enclosure," for purposes of study, and was often observed by visitors pacing to and fro, paper and pencil in hand, and stopping occasionally to jot something down. That he was preparing his next sermon was the natural surmise. Quite as probably he was under the influence of the muse. One of his favourite walks was down Longcauseway, from the east end of the vicarage garden, and along Sands Lane—the broad path on the bank of the river leading towards Horbury, a parish in which a much more famous literary clergyman—the Revd. S. Baring Gould, M.A., Vicar of Lew Trenchard, Devon—was subsequently curate.

In 1810, when most of these strolls took place, the Calder was a pellucid stream beloved of anglers. What it has since become let us briefly show by relating what took place at an official enquiry held a few years ago at Dewsbury.

One of the witnesses produced a bottle of supposed ink, and wrote with the fluid the word, Calder, on a sheet of foolscap which he handed to the Commissioner. "It is rather pale,' remarked the gentleman. "Yes," said the witness, "it is, but the bottle contains no ink; merely water from the river." The sample had been taken from near where Mr. Brontë used to stroll! The Commissioner made no further remark, but preserved the sheet, and in due time, when his report was issued in printed form, it was found that a *fac-simile* of "Calder" adorned one of the pages, pointing a moral, and also adorning the tale told at the public enquiry. There was added force in the fact that "Calder" means white river.

The gentleman did not explain from what particular black hole in the stream he had taken his sample, but it was shrewdly suspected that it had been drawn from the mouth of the beck, which, rising in Birkenshaw, flows down the valley past Birstall, Batley, and Soothill, and through the more thickly populated part of Dewsbury, a district where mills and dyeworks, if not "as thick as leaves in Valombrosa," are certainly very numerous.

CHAPTER V.

MR. BRONTË AS A CLERGYMAN—COTTAGE VISITING—DEALING WITH "ASSERTIVE IGNORANCE"—TENANTS OF THE ALDAMS —INTERESTING LETTER—VISITING OLD FRIENDS AT NAB END, SOOTHILL.

Let us see how Mr. Brontë performed his duties as a clergyman whilst in the parish of Dewsbury. We know that he was ordained in 1806 and went to the Essex curacy, remaining till 1809. We next, and only recently, hear of him at Wellington, where—states the vicar, the Revd. M. Marsh-Edwards, M.A., in reply to an enquiry we addressed to him this summer—he remained for about a year; probably for ten months or so; for the Dewsbury register books show that he had entered upon his duties here in December, 1809. On the 11th of that month he officiated at the marriage of one John Senior to a Miss Ellen Popplewell, both of Dewsbury, and signed the entry "P. Brontë, curate." After that date his name frequently appears in the church books, but not as often as would be the case now, for in registering funerals no record was made, except of the date of the interment, and the name of the deceased, followed by the initial letter of the parish to which the person belonged.

Like his vicar, Mr. Brontë was of the Evangelical school. He was a frequent preacher from the "three-decker" pulpit that faced the high old pews filling the nave and aisles, but was not considered equal to Mr. Buckworth either as a speaker or thinker. Many of the congregation, however, soon became attached to him, and the feeling spread amongst the people, for he was recognised as a truly earnest man, who did good work outside as well as inside the church. He was fond of catechising the children in church, and this was done once a month, the scholars of the Wesleyan Sunday School (who came each Sabbath day) attending with the others to be examined. Their singing, and that of the congregation, was led by a body of instrumentalists, and amongst them were two or three men who, in their own persons, and in those of sons, made their mark in the commercial life of the West Riding, then showing itself through the growth of the woollen manufacture. He also liked to hold cottage meetings (work shared by his vicar) and dropping in at this or that cottage the words from one of the dwellers to her neighbours: "Mr. Brontë is here," would bring many into the kitchen, or "house,"—as the living room was, and still is, styled in the district—and then would follow an earnest prayer meeting.

Though somewhat austere, Mr. Brontë was much liked by those swift and often correct readers of character, little children, and not seldom his familiar acquaintance with boy or girl, led the way to a friendship with the parents, and to frequent visits to their cottage, which he seldom left without offering prayer and praise. He delighted to work in the Sunday schools, and taking him all in all, it must be owned that he was at least a good average clergyman; and it is not surprising, but indeed was to be expected, that when the living of Hartshead-cum-Clifton fell vacant, as it did through the death of the Revd. W. H. Lucas, B.A., Mr. Buckworth, in whose gift it was, made the presentation to the curate who had served him so well during his stay in Dewsbury, albeit that curate—to use a common phrase in all manufacturing districts—had gone on strike, so far as preaching was concerned.

Mr. Brontë, though holding a subordinate position was a great power in the town. This came from the proofs he had given of lofty courage, sobriety, high principle, and true piety. That there were defects in his character goes without saying—goes without saying with all of us; they were, however, of such a character as tended to endear him to the homely folk amongst whom his lot was cast. He was exceedingly intolerant of assertive ignorance, and quickly, if not too kindly, perhaps, put it down; doing so all the speedier if the person exhibiting it was one of the well-to-do.

He certainly was not a favourite with men of what were called extreme views in politics—the moderates of to-day—and they were apt to let it be seen that they looked down upon the Irish curate. Doubtless he could not see that they had attained the moral or intellectual elevation that would enable them to "look down," so far as he was concerned, and there was no love lost between them. The bent of his mind politically was distinctly Tory, so was his training after he left Ireland, whatever it was before that time, but he sympathised deeply with the working classes, who, because of bad laws at home and the dislocation of trade through the gigantic and long-continued war on the Continent, were in a grevious state of poverty, being ill-fed and clad and poorly paid, a condition in which they unfortunately long remained.

When making enquiries some years ago into Mr. Brontë's connection with the parish—enquiries patiently conducted and long continued—we were told, and published the statement, that the revd.

gentleman "did not seek to cultivate the acquaintance of the wealthier people of Dewsbury, not even that of leading members of the congregation; indeed he repelled some advances that were made and gave offence to would-be entertainers." This, though true in the main, needs to be modified. We have learnt since, that very soon after his arrival he formed an acquaintance with the Hallileys, a family of note, and was a frequent visitor at their residence, The Aldams. The head of the house was known locally as "King of Dewsbury," a title conferred partly in derision. It was through him Mr. Brontë ceased to occupy the pulpit of the Parish church sooner than would otherwise have been the case, as we shall show in another chapter.

About seven years ago, when renewing enquiries made previously in several quarters as to the revd. gentleman's life and character, we received the following letter from a Dewsbarian—Mr. Halliley's successor in The Aldams—who took great interest in the affairs of the town of which he was a native, and who had retired to a pleasant Lancashire watering place, there to enjoy well-earned repose in the evening of his days. We allude to Mr. Mark Newsome, ex-mayor of Dewsbury, who, it will be seen, had named his new residence after the one in which he had spent so many years:

Aldams, 22, Albert Road, Southport,

November 25th, 1890.

Dear Sir,

I enclose a sheet statement respecting the Revd. P. Brontë, and hope that my delay in not forwarding it sooner has not caused you any inconvenience.

Yours truly,

(Signed) MARK NEWSOME.

"At the time the Revd. P. Brontë was curate at the Parish church, Dewsbury, viz., 1809 to 1811, Hanging Heaton formed part of the district the clergy had to visit, the church at Hanging Heaton not then being built. I have often heard my mother speak about the clergy calling at Nab End, the residence of my grandfather, Mr. Marmaduke Fox. He always spoke of Mr. Brontë as a very earnest man, but a little peculiar in his manner. My father, Mr. T. Newsome, and my uncle, Mr. Joseph Newsome, of Batley Carr, were well acquainted, and indeed intimate with Mr. Brontë. Both were regular attendants at the Dewsbury Parish Church during the time he was curate."

Subsequent investigations enable us to state that, with Mr. and Mrs. Marmaduke Fox, of Nab End, Soothill, he was a decided favourite, the revd. gentleman's efforts on behalf of the young Nowell—mentioned in another chapter—making the acquaintance already formed an intimate one. Both went to see Mr. and Mrs. Brontë soon after their marriage, and the young couple returned the visit, meeting several Dewsbury friends. The erstwhile curate and his wife also saw Mr. and Mrs. Buckworth at the Dewsbury Vicarage more than once in the first year of their marriage, and presumably received them at Hightown.

CHAPTER VI.

A STIRRING ADVENTURE—RESCUE OF A DROWNING BOY—ONLY "PICKED" INTO THE RIVER—MR. BRONTË'S COURAGE AND PROMPTITUDE.

Though Mr. Brontë's stay in Dewsbury was not a long one, it was marked with stirring incidents, as will be seen. One of these was during the winter of 1809-10. Early in an afternoon he left the vicarage, where he then lodged, for a stroll along the bank of the Calder, and taking a westerly direction came to Water Lane, a reputed Roman road, and here he had a somewhat startling adventure; one in which he exhibited the characteristics so marked in him of courage and promptness. Our informant, the son of a local tradesman, who at the time Mr. Brontë met him and a knot of playfellows, was a lad of about twelve years of age, told us that his father and companions had been to the long weir on the Calder, at the south-west end of the township, known as the broad dam, and were returning home. The weather was favourable, but rain had fallen for a few days previously, and the river was in flood. With them was an older boy of rather weak intellect, and they were amusing themselves by trying to recover from the swiftly flowing stream—then almost bank high—some of the pieces of wood that were floating down, he assisting. They had a long cord with a lump of iron at one end—a sort of grapnel—but it did not prove of much service, so they threw it away, and some of them commenced to teaze the half-imbecile.

There was no fence at the place where they happened to be, merely a few bushes at the river's brink. Just then a tall gentleman came up and passed, but took little if any notice of the youthful party. He had, however, not got more than ten or a dozen yards away before one of the lads—"I believe it was my father," said our informant—gave a rather hard push to the weak-headed boy, who, to the horror of all, fell into the water and was instantly battling for life. They screamed, and the gentleman, turning, ran back, and plunged into the flooded and swiftly-flowing river, and succeeded, though with evident difficulty, in reaching the drowning boy and bringing him to the bank. He then placed him on the path, his companions standing at some distance, afraid and yet pleased; and having tended him there, carried him to the cottage of his mother, a poor widow at Dawgreen—then a suburb, and now part of the town of Dewsbury—one of the unfortunate lad's companions showing the way, and the others following at some distance.

Mr. Brontë stayed a short time in the cottage—doubtless whilst the victim of the prank was being put to bed – and then parting with the widow at the door, set off for the vicarage. The other lads, frightened at what had occurred, and reluctant to go to their several homes, had loitered near, and were met by him. Who the rescuer was they could not then tell—he was hatless and wet through, but they now recognised him as the curate of the Parish Church. Mr. Brontë was plainly shivering, yet he stopped in his hurried walk, having recognised them, to lecture the party on their conduct, and especially the chief offender. This lad excused himself by saying, "I only picked (pushed) him, to make him wet his shoon," whereupon the parson's stern expression of face relaxed, and smiling, he bade them go to the widow's cottage to ask her pardon and that of her unfortunate son. They eagerly promised to do so, and then he strode off, changed his walk to a run, and was soon out of sight.

Mr. Brontë had not asked who did the ill deed to the mentally weak boy. The culprit disclosed himself, and his frankness, though covered with an excuse, dissipated any anger the revd. gentleman might have felt; that, and the knowledge that he had saved the life of a fellow creature. It was the opinion of the lads, who, of course, watched Mr. Brontë's movements in the water with anxiety and trepidation, that he could not swim. Be that as it may, he hesitated not a moment, but rushing into the swirling flood, was fortunate in seizing the widow's son and bringing him to the side about twenty yards below the place where he had been " picked " in.

CHAPTER VII.

MR. BRONTË AND THE BELL RINGERS—STOPPING THE PEAL—HIS REMOVAL FROM THE VICARAGE—THE ANCIENT WELL HOUSE—"OLD STAFF"—MR. BUCKWORTH A TRAINER OF MISSIONARIES—WHO SOME OF THEM WERE.

Another anecdote about him, the particulars of which were collected several years ago, will no doubt be relished, exhibiting Mr. Brontë in a characteristic light. One Sunday evening, having concluded the service in church, he returned to the vicarage and sat down in his study to rest; but, as it transpired, not for long. The worshippers had been called to church in the usual way, and no one, and he least of all, expected to hear the bells again ring. But they were, and to his very great astonishment. The vicar was away, and the ringers, knowing that, thought they would be able to have a practice-peal undisturbed; for a contest with men from church towers in other towns was to take place on the morrow.

They had not taken the curate into account at all, but he soon let them know somebody was in charge. Seizing his favourite stick, an Irish shillalagh, he darted out of the room, made for the house of Thomas Smith, the parish clerk, and enquiring why the bells were being rung, was told of the coming competition.

The news incensed Mr. Brontë very greatly. Ringing the bells for such a purpose was a desecration of the Sabbath, and that he would not permit any longer. He accordingly obtained the keys, ran to the church, hastily ascended the winding steps of the tower, and brandishing his weapon, stopped the astonished ringers, and drove them out, giving all a stern admonition, which they would interpret as "dare to do the like again." Smith, too, was reproved, for the ringing had taken place with his connivance, and by arrangement he had locked the ringers in.

Next morning the men waited upon Mr. Brontë. They had recovered courage and were highly indignant. They told him of the series of contests that were soon to commence, and explaining that they were not in a state of preparedness, and saw no harm, seeing that service was over for the day, and they had fulfilled their duties, why they could not have had an hour's practice. He was very severe with them, so severe that one ringer declared he would never enter the tower again until Mr. Brontë apologised. The man kept his word; he gave up

THE REVD. P. BRONTË, B.A., 1809.

his position, and was never afterwards seen in the ringing chamber. He also left the church, but returned in a few weeks, and became what he never was before, a devout member of the congregation.

We have named that Mr. Brontë had a shillalagh, and that it was his favourite stick. When at Hartshead it, or one of the same kind, was his companion, and the mode of carrying it led to him being jocularly spoken of by Mr Atkinson and Mr. Hammond Roberson as "Old Staff." This Mrs. Hirst well remembers as being a common expression.

It does not appear to have been known why Mr. Brontë left the Dewsbury vicarage. Quitting it after some months' pleasant residence, he went to lodge at what was known, because of an antiquarian discovery, as the Ancient-Well House, in Priest Lane —the present Church Street—not more than forty yards or so from Mr. Buckworth's. The Ancient-Well House was the property of the Carrett family, whose head was Mr. Elliot Carrett, an attorney of considerable repute in the district, and who, as the parish books show, greatly interested himself in town's affairs. Mr. Carrett was born in 1789, and died at the comparatively early age of forty-seven. Whether he resided at the house named when Mr. Brontë lodged there we do not know.

His daughter, who married a Mr. Jackson and

went to reside at Sheffield, a philanthropic lady, kindly furnished us with some information, and we learnt that her father considered Mr. Brontë "clever and good-hearted, but hot-tempered, and in fact, a little queer."

Why did Mr. Brontë leave Mr. Buckworth's roof, seeing that the vicarage was a commodious structure —at all events considered so in those days—and the two men on friendly, and indeed affectionate terms? This is a question not easy of solution after the lapse of time; but we think one may be found. Mr. Buckworth had undertaken to do something towards training young men who were afterwards to be ordained and go abroad—chiefly to India—as agents of the Church Missionary Society. Among them was Mr. Benjamin Bailey, of Dewsbury, who had a most useful and distinguished career. The official record says—"1812. Two years under the Revd. T. Scott, one year under the Revd. J. Buckworth, vicar of Dewsbury" Another of the vicar's pupils was Mr. Thos. Dawson, of Wakefield, and there must have been others, for many years ago when collecting materials for a history of the parish—more than a hundred and eighty chapters of which we published in the *Dewsbury Reporter*—we were informed by the venerable Mr. Samuel Oates, formerly a hat manufacturer in the town, that Mr. Buckworth "opened a sort of college in his house." It was attended by young men anxious to become missionaries to the heathen. Some were formerly scholars at the Parish Church school. After being ordained they spent part of their time in practical work, and then were sent out—chiefly to India.

Among these was Mr. Wm. Greenwood, who from 1810 to 1813 was under the Revd. T. Scott already named. It is recorded that he was the first clergyman of the Church of England sent as a missionary to India. Four missionaries and six young women, missionaries' wives, went out from the congregation of Dewsbury Parish Church up to 1811, as proved by extracts from the vicar's journal, published in vol. 14, p. 49 of *The Cottage Magazine*. In the same volume, pages 9 to 18, is a sermon preached by the Revd. Patrick Brontë.

CHAPTER VIII.

MR. BRONTË AND A VILLAGE BULLY—ENCOUNTER AT EARLSHEATON—WHAT DR. WRIGHT SAID—HIS NARRATIVE—DOUBTS CLEARED UP—STATEMENTS OF EYE WITNESSES—MR. BRONTË IN THE HOME CIRCLE—HIS INFLUENCE SEEN THEREIN.

"Ah! is not that the echo of something that happened in the sister country?" asked a gentleman who had been reading Dr. Wm. Wright's book, *The Brontës in Ireland*, when it was related to him how Mr. Brontë had dealt with a notorious bully near the village of Earlsheaton; which, situated on a hill, is distant but half a mile or so as the crow flies, from Dewsbury Old Church. The connection of the place with the mother parish, ecclesiastically and socially, as well as in trade, is close, and so far as local records extend, always has been; and there are not wanting indications that in years to come there may be a more intimate union. "Tell me," repeated the person referred to, "is not that the echo of something that happened in the Emerald Isle?" "It certainly is not," was our reply. "Whatever may have happened in Ireland, this was an actual occurrence on Yorkshire soil, as several eye-witnesses have testified." He expressed his desire to have further particulars of so interesting and unusual an occurrence and we gave him in the main the facts set out further on in the chapter.

Dr. Wright's narrative, describing what took place when Mr. Brontë was a teacher at Drumballyroney—presumably in 1799—is this:

"One little affair showed the metal of which he was made. He was leading the united Sunday and day school out for a holiday's amusement. The bully of the neighbourhood, a Roman Catholic, stood in the middle of a narrow path, and obliged the children to go down into a muddy ditch, to get past him. Patrick was coming past with Mr. Tighe, but on observing the conduct of the bully he broke away from the vicar, regardless of remonstrance, and seizing the offender by the neck and leg, flung him down the hill into the ditch, and left him there. This incident formed the groundwork of the story told by Charlotte in *Shirley*, where Helstone precipitated a similar obnoxious person into the ditch. Mr. J. A. Erskine Stuart tells, on the authority of Mr. Yates, a similar story of an event that took place on Whit Tuesday, 1810, at Earlsheaton. I am inclined to believe that the simple and sudden collision in Drumballyroney was the genuine original of all the later versions."

Which was the "genuine original" occurrence we do not propose to discuss, and will merely remark that we published an account of what occurred at Earlsheaton several years before Dr. Wright's book was given to the world, and that now, in printing fuller particulars, we furnish ample proof of the authenticity of the narrative:

On Monday or Tuesday in the Whitsun week of 1810 the scholars and teachers of the Sunday schools connected with Dewsbury Parish Church walked in procession through the principal streets of the town, as had been the custom for a few years—a custom kept up to the present time—and then proceeded to Earlsheaton, there to have what was locally known as "the sing," this taking place in an open space in the centre of the village called the Town's Green. These yearly visits were continued till 1829, before which time a church had been built and opened, and Sunday schools on a small scale established.

In the function of 1810, as in those preceding and following, much interest was taken by the church-people of the parish, and it was a subject of regret that the vicar of Dewsbury was too unwell to be present. His place was filled by the curate, Mr. Brontë, who doubtless had the assistance, as has been rendered for more than half a century, of the churchwardens, some of them Soothill men. Having completed the perambulation of the principal streets of the town, the processionists, girls leading, proceeded up Wakefield road, turning off at Dewsbury Bank, and following the highway leading to the village of Earlsheaton. Soon the scarp of the hill overlooking the beautiful valley of the Calder was reached, and a familiar landscape opened out to view, and doubtless was enjoyed, for bright sunshine illumined everything.

The young people, their teachers, and others walked merrily on, but in a moment were rudely interrupted, for a tall and strongly-built man, nearly forty years of age, and who, it was evident, was not quite sober, left the causeway on which he had been standing with some companions, and placing himself in front of the column, and spreading out his arms, told the girls, with an oath, that all must go back to Dewsbury, for he did not intend to let them pass. There was a sudden stoppage, of course, and a few cries of alarm. Mr. Brontë, who was a dozen yards or so from the front of the procession, hearing these, hurried up, and taking in the situation at a glance, and seeing that obstruction was fully meant, seized the ill-conditioned fellow by the collar, and with one effort flung him to the side of the road from whence he had come, and then, having restarted the scholars on their way, resumed his place at the side of the column as if nothing unusual had happened.

The obstructionist had not anticipated any such treatment; he was surprised and astounded, and his self-love was hurt, for had he not been "taken down" in the sight of many persons, among them his own boon companions, who were not sparing of ridicule? The fellow, however, soon recovered himself, and vowed that when the procession returned he "would hev it aat w't parson," meaning that he intended to be revenged on Mr. Brontë.

The affair caused not a little excitement, and the children, as they gathered on the village green, seemed too frightened to sing; but the revd. gentleman and his helpers calmed their fears, and the hymns were rendered with fervour if not with spirit. Quite a large assembly listened to their efforts, led as the voices were by a couple of stringed instruments played by men who officiated in "the singers' loft" in the parish church, which at that time was destitute of an organ.

When the time came for returning to Dewsbury there was again some trepidation, especially amongst the girls, for they feared (as did many women of the village) that Mr. Brontë would be attacked and beaten by the bully and his companions—well-known rough fellows—and they clustered round the curate.

He smilingly bade all put away their fears, and re-forming the procession, with the girls again leading, placed himself at its head and made for Dewsbury, where "the afternoon drinkings" awaited them. Men and lads of the village had ran forward to secure positions on the hill-side near where the encounter took place, fully expecting that a second and more serious one would follow.

In a few minutes the head of the procession approached the spot, and it was seen with alarm that the big man was on the causeway as before, and his friends also. Mr. Brontë passed calmly on, though watchful, then stopped as the children walked along, the man scowling, but saying nothing, and remaining on the path. Mr. Brontë, before resuming his place at the side of the procession, waited to see that the boys in the rear were not molested, and had the satisfaction of knowing that the bully had been effectually cowed. The man evidently considered "discretion the better part of valour;" what his companions thought about his conduct is not known. Perhaps they had acted as peacemakers, restraining him from "hevvin it aat w't parson."

Because of the doubt expressed as to this occurrence having actually happened, we think it advisable to state how the information came to our knowledge, and in what way, corroboration has been given. Mr. Joseph Newsome, of Carlton Grange, Batley, a gentleman with whom we were acquainted for several years, gave the first particulars, doing so on being told that on searching the Dewsbury parish church registers for historical items we had come across the name of Patrick Brontë. He knew a good deal about the revd. gentleman, and was willing and indeed anxious to impart such knowledge as he was possessed of. This narrative of the encounter between the man at Earlsheaton and Mr. Brontë he had had from old people, and one of these he fetched in his carriage from Soothill, a man named Senior, who fully corroborated Mr. Newsome's story, and, being questioned, furnished a few additional facts.

The bully, he said, belonged to Gawthorpe, a hamlet in the township of Ossett, and was a notorious cockfighter and boxer, and much addicted to drinking. Some of the men he was with on the memorable day were persons of like character.

Mr. Senior stated that he himself was one of the scholars of the Sunday School and was regularly taught both to read and write—secular as well as religious knowledge being imparted to the children in those comparatively dark days—and that Mr. Brontë was frequently one of his instructors. The old man was asked, did he see the actual flinging of the Gawthorpe man across the road, and he replied "No, I was lower down in the procession, the girls being first; but what happened was soon known by all of us"—as indeed it would be—"and we talked about it for many a Sunday." "What sort of a teacher was Mr. Brontë" we enquired, and Mr. Senior replied, "I can hardly say, I was but a little lad. He was resolute about being obeyed, but was very kind, and we always liked him."

It will interest at least local readers to know that Mr. Samuel Dawson, stationer, of Dewsbury, who for more than half a century was connected with the Parish Church Sunday School, as scholar, teacher, and superintendent, informed us some time before his death, that he had often conversed with ex-scholars who had been in the memorable procession, and witnessed the prompt action of the impetuous curate.

CHAPTER IX.

FURTHER CORROBORATION—"THE STORY TOLD IN *SHIRLEY*"—MR. BRONTË AND HIS CHILDREN—HIS INFLUENCE SEEN IN THEIR WRITINGS—MRS. GASKELL'S STATEMENT ON THAT POINT.

A word or two in further corroboration and then we pass on to other incidents in the revd. gentleman's life in Dewsbury. When an outline of this narrative was first published in the newspaper with which we were connected, Mr. Wilson Hemingway, a well-known resident, came to us, and said he had been greatly interested in its perusal, "for," he remarked, "my mother, then a Miss Wilson, and the daughter of a manufacturer at Dawgreen, was one of the processionists, and an eye-witness of what took place. She was a girl of eleven years of age at the time, and the occurrence made a deep impression on her mind." Mr. Hemingway added, "my mother often talked to me and the rest of her children about the Revd. Patrick Brontë, and told us more than once of the big rough man that would not let the procession of scholars pass, and that the revd. gentleman coming hastily up, flung him to the side of the road." Further, in conversation, Mr.

Hemingway said that his mother informed them that all were allowed to return to Dewsbury unmolested by the man.

This action on the part of Mr. Brontë was quite characteristic, and when it became known in Dewsbury—and the news quickly spread—it won him the commendation of the townspeople. "The Irish curate," as he was often styled, had proved his courage by saving the life of the Dawgreen boy, and this occurrence coming so soon after that action, the West Riding heart went out to the man; in an undemonstrative way, perhaps, but nevertheless in a manner that would convince him he had made more friends amongst those amid whom he was labouring than he had ever anticipated.

The story told in *Shirley* of the collision between the two processions, and the action of Mr. Helstone, if it has any foundation in fact, is far more likely to have had its origin in what took place near Earlsheaton than in what occurred at Drumballyroney.

"How came these girls—Charlotte and Emily in particular—to obtain the knowledge they possessed of West Riding people and West Riding ways?" has often been asked by readers of their novels. Well, they had the insight of genius, and possessed wonderfully keen perceptive powers, and though they sought no acquaintances amongst the strongly marked characters living in and about Haworth, they were observant always, and good listeners to Tabby, their father, and others, with whom they were brought into contact. Charlotte had many opportunities of improving her knowledge of human nature; for example, in her visits to Birstall and Gomersal, and during her residence at Mirfield, and at Dewsbury Moor, as well as Brussels, &c., and what she heard and saw would be stored away in the recesses of her mind, even if she did not make notes for future reference.

Then, her father! He was fond of talking to his children, and unconsciously to himself and to them, was being studied. He led them to "sympathise with him," says Mrs. Gaskell, "in his great interest in politics," lifting them "above the chances of their minds being limited or tainted by petty local gossip;" and who can doubt that he told them of people he had met and of scenes in which he had been an actor or an eye-witness.

The gifted biographer also tells us "their father was in the habit of relating to them any public news in which he felt an interest, and from the opinions of his strong and independent mind they would gather much food for thought," &c. He was a greater educator of his girls than many have given him credit for, and he himself was studied as well as the lessons he imparted. Like true artists in various walks of life, they not only created characters, but formed others, taking the materials from the strongly marked peculiarities of those around them. The subject is of great interest, and it can best be dealt with by writers more familiar than we are with the life of the wondrous family at Haworth.

CHAPTER X.

A MEMORABLE YEAR—LORD PALMERSTON AND MR. BRONTË—FALSE ENLISTMENT—SUFFERINGS OF A DEWSBURY YOUNG MAN—TREACHERY OF AN ACQUAINTANCE—COMING TO THE RESCUE—PALMERSTON'S LETTER TO THE DEWSBURY CURATE.

The year 1810 was a memorable one for Mr. Brontë, as we shall further show, by giving some particulars of an effort he made in conjunction with a few Dewsbury worthies to secure the release of an unjustly imprisoned young man, who was suffering through the falsehood of a fellow townsman, presumably an acquaintance. Before proceeding to furnish the details of a very remarkable case, we have to express our acknowledgments to the editor of the *Leeds Mercury* for permission to search the pages of that journal for 1810—11, and take extracts therefrom; and to the editor of the *Yorkshire Post* for facilitating our endeavours to examine those of the *Leeds Intelligencer* for the same years. Our thanks are also due to Mr. Newsome of Eccles, journalist, who placed us in possession of a copy of the first-named newspaper for December 15th, 1810, containing a long and succinct narrative in the form of a letter addressed to the editor, and which, though bearing at foot merely the *nom de plume* "Sydney," we have good reason for believing was from the pen of Mr. Brontë. Because of the interesting circumstances disclosed, and for the reason too that the communication throws much light upon his character, and not a little upon the times, we give the main portion to the public.

It is common knowledge that when Mr. Brontë was at Cambridge University, Lord Palmerston was there also, a member, like himself, of St. John's College; they in fact must have often been brought into contact. Those were troublous times. War was raging on the Continent, the great contest in which so much British blood was shed, and British gold spent, and which only came to an end with the decisive battle of Waterloo, in 1815. Englishmen had reason to believe that their "tight little island" was regarded with a greedy eye, and themselves with aversion; and, as was done at a much later date, they formed corps of volunteers, and were armed with the best weapons of the day, and learnt military exercises, with the intention of being of real service should invasion be attempted. Besides, there was the moral influence—not so termed ninety years ago—of bodies of armed and trained citizens being ready to defend their country and to assist the regular forces; and so it came about that at Cambridge, as in other towns and cities, corps of volunteers were established. It may be safely taken for granted that, ardent Tory as he was, and full of martial spirit, Mr. Brontë, a man of thews and sinews, and of many inches, soon offered himself, and was sworn in.

In the same company as himself was the young peer, his junior, but equally full of ardour and love of country, and almost as tall—Lord Palmerston. They drilled together of course, and probably formed some personal acquaintance, though of that we have no proof. If such was the case, they were destined to renew it for a short time, and whilst the former was in Dewsbury.

In 1806 both quitted the university, the young lord to contest the city, as he was anxious to obtain a seat in Parliament; the other to go to a sleepy agricultural parish as a curate. What a change in their careers! And what a contrast, subsequently! Palmerston fought and lost, and was unsuccessful in another constituency; then had an easy victory in a rotten borough, and entering the House of Commons, commenced almost at once a long and distinguished career, and for some years was Prime Minister. Mr. Brontë went from curacy to curacy, viz.:—from Weathersfield to Wellington, and thence to Dewsbury, where he stayed two years, leaving under somewhat remarkable circumstances, as we shall show in another chapter. Promoted by his vicar to the incumbency of Hartshead, as quiet a place almost as that amongst the Essex meadows, he did his work, and then exchanged for Thornton, a partly moorland parish, finally settling down at Haworth, where there were many square miles of moors at his very doors, and where he became known to the world at large, and then only through his daughters.

The young patrician saw life under very different conditions. He sought and obtained office, and though raw and untrained for such an enormously responsible post, had conferred upon him by the King the portfolio of Secretary at War. This was whilst Mr. Brontë was at Dewsbury, and the statesman and the humble curate were brought for a brief time officially together by correspondence.

Shortly before "Sydney's" narrative saw the light, a paragraph appeared in the *Mercury* of the 10th of November, 1810, stating that "a very industrious and respectable young man of the name of William Nowell, of Dewsbury, in this neighbourhood," was lying in the House of Correction at Wakefield, having been committed on the 25th of September on a charge of deserting from the 30th regiment, after enlistment "at Lee Fair, about four miles from Dewsbury, whereas no such enlistment had taken place, and he had not been at Lee Fair." The editor, remarking upon this, said, "This young man's case ought to awaken public sympathy, and we cannot doubt, call forth the humane interference of our county members."

One of these gentlemen was Lord Milton, the other the famous philanthropist and liberator of the slave, Wm. Wilberforce. Both seem to have interested themselves on behalf of Nowell, Mr. Wilberforce being particularly active, as will be seen. On the 1st of December the *Mercury* contained further reference to the case, and on the 15th of the same month the editor published the letter of "Sydney," fully two columns in length, giving an extended narrative of what had happened, and showing how an unjustly incarcerated, an innocent youth, had been released from prison and matters put in train for ensuring the adequate punishment of his oppressor.

We learn from the letter, and information published in the *Leeds Intelligencer*, in a report of a trial at Lammas York Assizes—for so the term runs—that a young Dewsbury man named James Thackray, who had enlisted in the 30th regiment, then stationed at Wakefield, made the assertion to the soldiers that he had enlisted a fellow townsman, one William Nowell, a young cloth weaver, the son of Mr. Thomas Nowell, of Dawgreen. There was a girl of his acquaintance named Love Webster, and Thackray declared that she knew of the taking of the enlistment shilling by Nowell; but there was only his word for it, and as events proved, that was of no worth whatever. The date of alleged enlisting on the part of Nowell, was the 18th of September, and the place, as stated, Lee Fair, otherwise Woodchurch, in the township of West Ardsley, where the second great horse fair of the year, and known to the present day as "the Latter Lee," was being held. If the youth had taken the shilling—and Thackray told the military authorities he had given him such a coin, and had formally enlisted him—it would have been Nowell's duty to have presented himself at the regimental headquarters, then in Wakefield, and as he did not appear, a party of soldiers was sent for him to the house of Mr. Nowell, senr. He was in, and on learning the errand, told the soldier in charge that he knew nothing of what they asserted, and that he had not enlisted, and certainly had not been to Lee Fair. His parents had, but he stayed in Dewsbury, and he declared he was able to account for his time. That, however, did not satisfy the colonel of the regiment when the report was made, and on the following day the youth was apprehended, conveyed to Wakefield, and taken before Mr. Dawson, J.P., where he was charged with desertion, and where Thackray, himself only a recruit, swore as to the enlistment. For the defence Mr. Nowell, senr., called seven inhabitants of Dewsbury, who deposed that the young man was in the town on the day in question, and not at Lee Fair, and the coroner (Mr. Brook, of Wakefield) and Mr. Nowell, sen., offered to send two post-chaises for more witnesses, but Mr. Dawson refused to consent, and committed the accused to the House of Correction as a deserter.

CHAPTER XI.

FURTHER INCIDENTS—THE DEWSBURY CURATE AND HIS FRIENDS GET A RE-HEARING—YOUNG NOWELL DISCHARGED—LETTER OF LORD PALMERSTON TO MR. BRONTË—THE PERJURER TRANSPORTED.

In the narrative from which we have quoted it is stated that "when the party returned to Dewsbury, and the result of their interview was made known, the astonishment and disappointment of the inhabitants was universal," "and that more than a dozen people came forward and were ready to make oath to having seen him (Nowell, jun.) in Dewsbury from one o'clock till the time he went to bed." On the Friday following, four gentlemen (one Mr. Brontë) waited upon Mr. Dawson, and having stated what further facts could be proved, asked him to revise the decision; but he refused, and accordingly a memorial to the Commander-in-Chief was prepared and forwarded, "signed by the clergymen, the churchwardens, and the principal inhabitants of Dewsbury," and this was accompanied by a letter, written, we believe, by Mr. Brontë; for, the narrative goes on, a reply was received in which it was said, "the clergyman was requested to state, for the information of the Secretary at War, whether the facts alleged in the memorial were to his own knowledge true, or if they were only believed to be so, and if so, to state the grounds of that belief." Mr Brontë was addressed personally and officially at the close of the remarkable proceedings, by the Secretary, Lord Palmerston.

A vestry meeting was called, and a second memorial forwarded, but the answer came that the Secretary "did not see that he could with propriety interfere with the decision of the civil magistrate in the case." "The public became more than ever concerned, and resolved that one of the city members should be seen, and Mr. Halliley, sen., of Dewsbury, manufacturer, who happened to be in London, went to the War Office, along with Mr. Wilberforce, and tried to get a re-hearing. They were permitted to apply to Mr. Dawson, and did so, through Mr. Maule, an eminent barrister, but the magistrate would not give way."

Mr. Wilberforce was indignant, and going again to the War Office, he succeeded in getting an imperative order calling upon the unwilling magistrate to re-hear the case, and to send up the evidence that it might be examined.

"Accordingly, the Revd. Mr. Brontë, Mr. Hague,

Mr. Halliley, jun., and Mr. Rylah (the latter a local attorney) attended on Mr. Dawson with fifteen witnesses." The magistrate remarked that they might have bought off the youth for £25, but he was told "they were not going to buy justice on those terms: that though an appeal to the proper tribunal was expensive, yet the redress was to be had, and that ten times £25—aye, and much more—would willingly be forthcoming to procure that redress, than the smallest sum to purchase his liberty."

The re-hearing then took place, and the witnesses "proved a most incontestible *alibi*," and, in addition, a Wakefield tradesman deposed to having heard Thackray confess that he had not enlisted Nowell at all, and had not seen him at Lee Fair. In five days afterwards—ten weeks' rigorous imprisonment having been undergone—Nowell, jun., was restored to his family.

"Sydney" (Mr. Brontë) showed in his letter to the *Mercury* how certain clauses in the Mutiny Act operated against the liberty of the subject, and saying that Lord Milton, as well as Mr. Wilberforce, had interested himself on behalf of young Nowell, informed the public that it was intended to prosecute Thackray; also to bring an action for false imprisonment against the committing magistrate, and closed with the following remarks: "It is a proud reflection and a source of consolation in these times that, while the iron hand of despotism is falling heavy on the continent of Europe, we Englishmen still enjoy the pure administration of justice; that we have laws to regulate the conduct of every man, from a beggar to a king; and that no station, however low, no rank, however high, can screen from justice him that doeth wrong."

That Mr. Brontë was a moving spirit in this matter—if not the actual leader—is clear from the following copy of a letter which the editor of the *Mercury* published with a few words of commendation on the course taken:

War Office, *5th December*, 1810.

Sir,

Referring to the correspondence relative to Wm. Nowell, I am to acquaint you that I feel so strongly the injury that is likely to arise to the service from an unfair mode of recruiting, that if by the indictment which the lad's parents are about to prefer against James Thackray they shall establish the fact of his having been guilty of perjury, I shall be ready to indemnify them for the reasonable and proper expenses which they shall bear on the occasion.

I am, sir,

Yours, &c.,

(Signed) PALMERSTON.

To the Revd. P. Brontë, Dewsbury, near Leeds.

To complete the history of this transaction we give the following from the *Mercury* of Saturday, the

10th of August, 1811.—"James Thackray, the soldier who was indicted for perjury for having falsely sworn that he enlisted William Nowell, of Dewsbury, at Lee Fair, on the 18th of September, 1810, took his trial in the criminal court at York, on Thursday last, and was convicted of the offence on the clearest evidence, to the satisfaction of the whole court." The editor added:—"We envy the feelings of those gentlemen whose public spirited and persevering conduct has secured to public justice a victory over the advocates and abbettors of this profligate delinquent; by their exertions a worthy young man has been restored to his family and friends, and the grey hairs of his aged parents have been rescued from an untimely grave, to which the outrage done to their only son was fast hastening them. We have already at some personal risk, brought the public acquainted with the facts of this nefarious transaction, and we shall not fail to seize the earliest opportunity to give the particulars of the trial."

Both that journal and the *Intelligencer* furnish reports of the trial, at which thirteen witnesses were called for the prosecution and five for the defence. It is not necessary to give the particulars, except to show how Nowell, jun., supported by the oaths of several people, accounted for his time on the day of the alleged enlistment. He said that Lee Fair day was a holiday at Dewsbury, and that his father and mother went to the fair about one o'clock, and he "went to warp a chain preparatory to weaving"—a statement which most readers living in the clothing district will readily understand; that he put the "chain" or warp into his loom, and continued in the workshop till 3 p.m. Afterwards, "there being an outcry that they were going to take up the body of Mr. Jackson, buried without a coroner's inquest"—about which more anon—"he went into the churchyard, amongst many others, to look on, and hearing that the raising was not to take place till six o'clock, he went into the market place," thence to Messrs. Halliley's mill, and he accounted for his time up to a late hour.

Among the witnesses for the defence was one George Blackburn, a soldier, who deposed to seeing Nowell, jun., at Lee Fair; but as to this man, Mr. Halliley, jun., was called, and he told the jury that when driving to York to attend the assizes he overtook Blackburn, to whom, on a complaint that he was very tired, he gave a lift in his gig, and that the soldier confessed to him that he had not seen Nowell, jun., there at all.

Thackray was found guilty and sentenced to seven years' transportation across the seas; but we do not learn that the equally perjured Blackburn, himself a Dewsbury man, was punished. The sentence imposed was a very severe one. Severity, however, characterised punishments under the criminal law, as witness the death penalty being inflicted on other convicted persons at the same assize, the offences being horse-stealing, rape, burglary, and the theft of a bill of exchange. Next day these awful sentences were commuted—to transportation for life!

CHAPTER XII.

HOW THE ALIBI WAS PROVED—A DEWSBURY TRADESMAN'S FREAK—IT ENDED IN A TRAGEDY—HIS DEATH AND THAT OF HIS WIFE—REPORTED SUICIDE—AN EXHUMATION—NOWELL IN THE CHURCHYARD WHEN THE SOLDIER SAID HE WAS AT LEE FAIR.

"Sydney," it will have been noticed, described the *alibi* set up on behalf of the young fellow, Nowell, as most incontestable. The revd. gentleman was right. It certainly was not of the class defined by a punning and sarcastic lawyer, as, "A lie by which many a rogue escapes hanging," the innocence of the youth being fully established and in a most remarkable manner.

It seems that on Sunday, the 2nd of August, 1810, Mr. S. M. Jackson, druggist, of Dewsbury, paid a visit to a friend in Rothwell jail, and returned in a state of intoxication on horseback. Seeing the door of a place of worship open he thought it fine fun to ride in, going near to the pulpit, and of course disturbing both minister and congregation. Some of the men seized the animal's head, led it into the street, and gave Mr. Jackson into custody and he was conveyed to prison. This would be to the curious, ancient, and incommodious structure demolished a few years ago by the Dewsbury Corporation when improving Vicarage Road, and which was known as Old Towzer. The news of his arrest and the circumstances that led to it quickly spread through the town and district, and caused much astonishment.

Mrs. Jackson was in Wakefield at the time, attending the funeral of her sister, and being told what had occurred she became greatly excited and returned to Dewsbury, where she was taken seriously ill. The poor lady was *enciente*, and the pains of labour coming on, she was prematurely confined, and to the horror of her friends, sank and died. Mr. Jackson was dismayed at the consequences of his folly, but little anticipated that they would include a deep domestic sorrow. The news of his wife's death was conveyed to the unhappy man and had a stunning effect. He became seriously unwell, was seized with a fit, and soon expired.

This double tragedy greatly affected the public mind, a painful sensation being caused all over the district; for, as the report says, "Mr. Jackson was much and deservedly respected," and this freak of his was put down to the drink and not to the man. Rumours were started to the effect that, dismayed and overpowered with horror at the death of his wife, he committed suicide. The interment of her remains was on the 5th of August, and the entry in the register of burials is simply that date, and "Martha, wife of Samuel Mark Jackson (D)," the terminal letter signifying that deceased belonged to Dewsbury. For the two contiguous townships in the parish the initial letters of Ossett and Soothill, respectively, appear in the book.

The funeral of the husband took place on the 14th, and doubtless both bodies were laid in the same grave. The register shows that there were two interments that day. This was the last and the only record of what all expected to be the final chapter in a sorrowful story, viz., "14th, Samuel Mark Jackson (D)."

Soon after the body had been laid in the ground the rumours were further spread abroad, and it was asserted again that he had died, not from a fit, but through taking poison. The statements were persistently repeated, and being strongly believed in, the local authorities decided to apply to the Secretary of State, in London, for an order of exhumation. This was obtained, either by the constable of Dewsbury or the coroner, and a *post mortem* examination was made, and the result laid before a jury at an inquest. The medical evidence was conclusive that the organs of the body were free from poison and that death had occurred from natural causes. Official notification was then made, as per the verdict of the jury, and the gossips being silenced if not abashed, the corpse was reinterred, and so ended the last scene in a tragedy of more than local interest.

In the ordinary course of his duty Mr. Brontë would conduct the funeral services over the bodies of the ill-starred pair, and he probably would be present at the reinterment of Mr. Jackson's remains. He therefore would be deeply interested, as will be seen, in the case of Nowell, junr., and resolve that no stone should be left unturned to secure his release and the punishment of the perjurer, Thackray.

But what of young Nowell? Could these remarkable proceedings bear in any way on his enlistment or non-enlistment? We shall soon see. The exhumation took place on latter Lee Fair day, the 18th of September—rather more than a month having elapsed since the burial—and that was the very day on which Thackray said the youth was enlisted, and to which day he swore before Mr. Dawson, the magistrate, of Wakefield. Nowell, jun., was, however, in Dewsbury, for a time in the churchyard (along with other morbidly minded sightseers, waiting to see Mr. Jackson's coffined body raised from the grave), and in other places in the town, and was noticed by several people who knew him well. It was their evidence, that of his father (who had been at the fair in question), and his own detailed statement, unshaken on cross-examination, that led the jury to return a verdict of guilty against Thackray, *vide* the report in the papers, without a moment's hesitation, and to his being transported for the long term ordered by the judge.

That Mr. Brontë took almost as great an interest in the trial of the perjurer as he did in securing the release of the innocent young man, may safely be assumed. Young Nowell resumed his avocation when the trial was over and followed it some time. Later in life he entered the employment of Messrs. Hagues, Cook, and Wormald, blanket manufacturers, of Dewsbury Mills, as a fuller, and we are told remained with the firm up to his death.

CHAPTER XIII.

A PARISH CLERK, HIS DEPORTMENT—ITS IMPORTANCE—MR. BRONTË HAS AN ASSISTANT CLERK—THEIR JOURNEYS TO AND FROM HARTSHEAD—MR. BRONTË INSULTED BY THE "KING OF DEWSBURY"—HE PREACHES FOR THE LAST TIME AT DEWSBURY—"WHAT! KEEP A DOG AND BARK HIMSELF."

When Mr. Brontë was curate at Dewsbury, the office of Parish Clerk was filled by Mr. Thomas Smith, ex-sexton, appointed in 1802, and who held office for about twenty-eight years. A curious deed contains a record, signed by himself, of what he undertook to perform. For example he said, *inter alia*, "I will give no notice of rent days, common day work, sales, or the like in the church, except such as required by law to be given there. All others I will cry afterwards at the church door. . . . As the deportment of the clerk is of great consequence, I solemnly promise to abstain from frequenting alehouses needlessly, and from tippling and drinking to excess, and other vices connected with such a practice, and that if ever I am drawn in, and overcome, I will submit to reproof from the minister or churchwardens."

In the later days of his engagement Smith was assisted by his son, John (afterwards clerk at St. John's, Dewsbury Moor, and subsequently at St. Peter's, Earlsheaton), and prior to that, when occasion required, by a young man named Joseph Tolson, who lived at Bridge End, Dewsbury, in one of a few cottages whose sites are occupied by the coal staiths and yard of the Lancashire and Yorkshire Railway Co. When about fourteen years of age, Tolson, according to the terms of a deed we recently had the opportunity of inspecting, was bound apprentice in 1806 to Mr. Joseph Ward, a small manufacturer, "to follow the occupation of a broad-cloth weaver." The indenture was of course signed by the contracting parties, and the attesting witnesses were Mr. John Ward and Mr. Samuel Chadwick.

Education was not the birthright of every child in those days, a knowledge of the three R's even was confined to comparatively few; but this deed bears no cross. It was signed by the boy, and in a very creditable hand. As to the occupation he was to follow, readers not belonging to the Yorkshire clothing districts might conclude from the stipulation in the deed of apprenticeship that Dewsbury competed with the West of England in the production of the fine fabrics then made there; but the term was understood to cover any class of textile woven in broad looms, and as a matter of fact Tolson's time was mostly taken up with the weaving of blankets. He followed this trade in his manhood for several years, and then gained more lucrative employment. He had married, and losing his wife in 1871, went to reside with his youngest daughter and her husband, and spent some time with them in the West of England, and at York, in which city he died in 1878.

We give these and other particulars (supplied by his grandson, Mr. John E. Tolson, and his daughter-in-law, Mrs. G. Tolson, both of Dewsbury) for the reason that he formed a rather close acquaintance with Mr. Brontë, and which extended over several years. Very soon after the revd. gentleman came to Dewsbury the youth became a singer in the choir, and took an interest in the church and Sunday school. He wrote fairly, could read well and with confidence, and with Mr. Buckworth's permission he was allowed to officiate for Smith on a few occasions when the latter was unwell.

At Hartshead, the oldest daughter-church, the Vicar was the Revd. W. H. Lucas, B.A., and his health was precarious. It therefore became necessary that he should have assistance at times in conducting divine worship, and this was given by Mr. Brontë. Those were not the days of surpliced choirs, and a large part of the service in any ordinary church consisted of little more than the saying of prayers and psalms by the parson, and the reading of the responses by the clerk. Who else officiated in the church of this remote and sparsely populated district is not known to us; the probability is that each clergyman that came to "supply" during Mr. Lucas's illness would bring some one with him. Mr. Brontë did so, and with the approval of his Vicar, no doubt, made choice of young Tolson. In going to and from the village each rode a cob, and in this way, conversing as they went, an acquaintance sprung up between them. Mr. Brontë appeared very happy at Dewsbury, but his feelings became quite changed through an occurrence which the young singer often referred to in later years.

It seems that one Sunday it had been arranged that Mr. Brontë should go to Hartshead and conduct service morning and afternoon, as he had done on previous occasions. Under ordinary circumstances he would, at night, have had little else to do at Dewsbury Parish Church than read some of the prayers. The Vicar however told him he wished to spend the Sunday evening at the Aldams, where his wife's relatives resided, the occasion being a family gathering, and he asked Mr. Brontë to take the entire service. No objection was made, and on the Sabbath morning he and Tolson rode off, and at Hartshead did what was required of them.

When returning to Dewsbury both were caught in a thunderstorm and drenched with rain. Mr. Brontë, instead of going to his rooms to effect a change of clothing, made speed for the Aldams, the young assistant following. On arriving he was met by Mr. Halliley, senr., to whom he explained that according to an arrangement made between himself and the Vicar he was to take the entire service, and that being wet to the skin, he wished Mr. Buckworth to officiate instead. On hearing this Mr. Halliley exclaimed, and very likely in jest, "What! keep a dog and bark himself."

Mr. Brontë saw no fun in the remark, but taking it to be a deliberate insult, was highly incensed. He, however, said not a word, but turning off abruptly left Mr. Halliley, the young man following. They soon had to part, however; each to go to his home for change of clothes and needed refreshment.

Tolson was curious to know what would be the upshot of this affair, and after tea he repaired to the Parish Church. Mr. Brontë was already there, and seemingly quite cool and collected. Prayers were gone through, the psalms said or sung, and the lessons read. Then in due course, and whilst a hymn was being rendered, Mr. Brontë ascended the higher stairs of the "three-decker" to deliver his sermon. If the congregation were at all sleepy that evening, they must soon have been aroused, for he announced that it was not his intention to preach again after that evening, giving as his reason that he had been most grievously insulted. The particulars were not vouchsafed, and there was naturally great surprise manifested amongst the assembled people. Mr. Brontë then gave out his text and preached a sermon of considerable power, but made no allusion in it to what had occurred but a short hour or so before at the Aldams.

The extraordinary incident formed the theme of conversation when service was over and the congregation dispersing. Mr. Brontë was as good as his word. That was his last discourse in Dewsbury Parish Church. He, however, officiated at a few marriages as the register book shows, and why he should have drawn the line at the pulpit seems rather curious.

What had occurred would be a grief and an annoyance to Mr. Buckworth. It however did not interfere with his friendship for the irascible curate, and very soon afterwards the living of Hartshead falling vacant it was conferred by him upon Mr. Brontë, no doubt in pursuance of a previous promise. It would seem that the regrettable incident at the

Aldams did not prevent Mr. Brontë and Mr. Halliley, junr. (who resided at Grove House, Dewsbury), working amicably together to secure the release from jail of the unfortunate youth, Wm. Nowell, whose case is mentioned in another chapter.

CHAPTER XIV.

THE IRISH AND THE YORKSHIRE CHARACTER CONTRASTED—MR. BRONTË AND A YOUNG WEAVER—"BRANWELL'S CHAIR" AT THE BLACK BULL, HAWORTH—ANOTHER RELIC—IS IT A "GENUINE ORIGINAL?"

We were informed when pursuing our investigations that Mr. Joseph Tolson often talked with his relatives about Mr. Brontë, and that they gathered from him that though rather reserved in manner, and apt to be abrupt in speech when strangers were present, he was chatty and agreeable with people with whom he had formed an acquaintance. This confirms what others had said about the revd. gentleman.

Says the Revd. M. Morris in his interesting book, *Yorkshire Folk-Talk*, "It is difficult to understand natures more opposite than those of the Irishman and the Yorkshireman; the quick, impulsive, excitable temperament of the Celtic character is utterly foreign to that of the Clevelander, or East Ridinger," and he might have added, or the West Ridinger; "A more practical people do not exist than Yorkshire people," remarks the same writer; and a man like

Mr. Brontë would but slowly make his way into their affections under ordinary circumstances; but the courage he displayed in saving the drowning lad, his promptness in dealing with the obstructionist at Earlsheaton, and the energy he showed, along with others, in going to the rescue of William Nowell, one of their own town's lads, would soon endear him to them, and cause them to forgive his hot temper and impulsiveness, especially as the actuating motive with him was always good.

"Mr. Brontë was a well informed man," was said by one who remembered him at Hartshead and Thornton, "and I always enjoyed his conversation" His learning and knowledge of the world gained in the humble schools in his native country, in the English university, and in his curacies, though not extensive, and indeed narrow and restricted, judged by the standard of to-day, placed him at a great advantage over most of the people he met with hereabouts, as well as at his subsequent places of residence.

The young weaver we have named was greatly interested in him, and often visited Mr. Brontë at Hartshead Church on Sundays, as did others of like age and similar occupation, who were connected with Dewsbury Parish Church, and all of whom he had taught in the Sunday school or schools, for much of the instruction would be given to girls and boys alike in houses, the occupation of rooms in which had been arranged for. At the village church these youths would see not only the parson they liked so well, but the somewhat fragile-looking bride Mr. Brontë brought to her new home in Hightown, Hartshead being without a vicarage; and some would doubtless see the two little ones born to the pair, Maria and Elizabeth, ere they quitted the parish. When the Brontë's removed to Thornton, on an exchange of livings being effected with the Revd. Thos. Atkinson, Mr. Tolson went over occasionally to see them, and he visited Mr. Brontë at Haworth more than once. The two had some correspondence, and the letters received by Mr. Tolson were preserved for a long time. What they contained or what became of them is not known to our informants.

One interesting relic Mr. John E. Tolson was able to show us whilst these chapters were being prepared for the press, viz., an old chair of peculiar shape, the property of his grandfather, who had it from a relative, and which it was always understood had come from the old vicarage of Dewsbury. He said "There were two of these chairs. I have heard my grandfather say more than once. He believed Mr. Brontë had the other, but what became of it neither my mother nor I know." We told him of one resembling it at the Black Bull Inn, Haworth, and the following day laid before him a picture of it in *The Sketch* of the 25th of May, 1895, a reproduction of a photograph. This was the piece of furniture known as "Branwell's Chair," and which some are of opinion came from the home of the erring young man. There does not, however, appear to be any ground for that view. Having written to Mr. W. Sugden, landlord of the Black Bull, on the subject, he wrote on the 26th ult., saying, "I am sorry I am not able to give you the full history of the chair. It was here in my grandparents' days. The chair did not belong to the Brontë family. Branwell Brontë used to sit in it in the room where the chair now is."

Kindly complying with a request made by us, Mr. Stead photographed the Dewsbury chair, as he had that at Haworth, for there are points of resemblance as well as differences of construction, the intention being to place pictures of both before the reader. Mr. Sugden's letter however renders this course unnecessary.

CHAPTER XV.

HARTSHEAD CHAPELRY—ANCIENT CUSTOMS—MR. BRONTË INDUCTED—HIS MARRIAGE—BIRTHS OF TWO CHILDREN—YOUNG DISCIPLES FROM DEWSBURY—HARTSHEAD REGISTERS—THE EXCHANGE OF LIVINGS—THE NEW VICAR AND HIS WIFE—CHARLOTTE BRONTË AT ROEHEAD—SHE VISITS HER GOD-PARENTS.

Turn we now to Hartshead—Hartshead-cum-Clifton, the larger parish was styled when Mr. Brontë was presented—where, crowning a hill running into much table-land north and easterly, stands an old house of prayer, dedicated to St. Peter, the oldest daughter-church of Dewsbury. The two were closely connected in the ancient Rectory; it may almost be said were united, and when the vicarage of Dewsbury was constituted in 1349 that union was mentioned, and was further strengthened in the deed made by William, Archbishop of York, on the 20th of June in that year, at his manor of Ripon. Then, Hartshead was a "chapell" only; now it is a vicarage, but the incumbent of the mother parish has rights and privileges, which, though some of them have fallen into disuetude, might perhaps be enforced; and has certain duties which the vicar of Hartshead could compel him to perform, resist he ever so stoutly. It is not likely, however, that the "auld warld" stipulations so carefully set out on parchment, will ever be insisted upon by either side; and that the clergymen will, for instance, quarrel over the washing of surplices, the finding of oil for the lamps, or the repairing of the books of prayer used by the Hartshead church-goers.

In Mr. Brontë's days, and subsequently, and prior, too, to the time when he set foot in the parish, St. Peter's was a wretched-looking building; but some years ago the fabric nnderwent restoration—work carried out with good judgment and carefulness, and the result is a pleasure alike to the parishioners and to archæologists The living was given to Mr. Brontë in 1811, and he was inducted on the 20th of July in that year. There was nothing for him but the church and churchyard, and a not too large congregation; both schools and parsonage being awanting; except that, as regards education, there was a free grammar school, founded in 1729 by Sir John Armytage, Bart., of Kirklees. It was customary for the Armytage family to appoint a master, who was often a curate.

Mr. Brontë did not take the office, nor, we are informed, did the Revd. Thos. Atkinson, M.A., with whom he exchanged livings in 1815; but after the death of the latter, the Revd. James Webb, M.A., curate of Dewsbury, who was appointed vicar in 1866, accepted the office in order that he might the better get the charity re-constituted, and gave the work and salary to a layman, who taught the three R's, and little more. A commodious national school was built in later days, but it is only during the incumbency of the present vicar, the Revd. Thos. King, M.A., formerly curate of Dewsbury, that a parsonage house was erected, a handsome and commodious structure, occupying a delightful position.

Mr. Brontë in his bachelor days lodged with Mr. and Mrs. Bedford, at Thorn-bush farm, and subsequently rented a house at the top of Clough Lane, Hightown, to which he brought the sweet and tender flower, his youthful Cornish bride, Maria Branwell. This would be early in January, 1813. Their marriage had taken place on the 29th of December, and, as there was a double event, we may perhaps be pardoned for reproducing the following from the *Gentleman's Magazine* for 1813, page 179:

" Lately, at Guiseley, near Bradford, by the Revd. W. Morgan, minister of Bierley, Revd. P. Brontë, B.A., minister of Hartshead-cum-Clifton, to Maria, third daughter of the late T. Branwell, Esq., of Penzance. At the same time, by the Revd. P. Brontë,

MARIA BRANWELL (AFTERWARDS MRS. P. BRONTË),
AT THE AGE OF 15 YEARS.

Revd. W. Morgan, to the only daughter of Mr. John Fennell, head-master of the Wesleyan Academy, near Bradford." The brides were cousins.

Whilst at the pro-parsonage, two children were born, Maria and Elizabeth Brontë. The baptism of the first was duly solemnised and entered in the Hartshead register book, the volume used being one in which the first record is dated January 10th, 1814. Reduced from the form, half printed, half written, the particulars given are:

"When baptised: April 23rd, in the church; Christian name: Maria, daughter of parents: the Revd. Patrick Brontë, minister of this church, and Maria his wife, Hartshead. By whom ceremony performed: Mr. Morgan, the officiating minister;" the latter the same who wedded the babe's parents and was himself married in December, 1812. Of the baptism of Elizabeth there is no mention in the register books of Hartshead, and it was only whilst this book was being printed that an official record was discovered. It was found in one of the volumes at Thornton Church by Mr. J. J. Stead. The entry is that Elizabeth, the daughter of Patrick and Maria Brontë, was baptised on the 26th August, 1815, and that the officiating minister was the Revd. J. Fennel. The ink is very pale; this had caused the writing to be previously overlooked by Mr. Stead and other searchers.

We have seen that Mr. Brontë whilst at Dewsbury was a diligent visitor, and held frequent meetings for praise and prayer at the houses of humble folk, and that he interested himself in other ways for the good of the community. Making enquiries at Hartshead some years ago we learnt that he pursued a similar course, and gave instruction to classes of young men in secular and religious knowledge. He also engaged in literary labour, completing for his first book, what he no doubt engaged in at Dewsbury.

It is a strong testimony to the value of his work in the mother parish, and to the loveableness of the impetuous man, that for several months after he left his curacy there, as we ascertained from Mr. Mark Newsome, it was quite common for youths he had taught in school or cottage to walk over to Hartshead on Sundays, to take part in the services in the quaint old church, and to hear their friend and late instructor preach. Out and home, the journey was about ten miles, but the distance was thought little of by these young disciples, who went and returned in a party, and always took food with them ere starting from their respective homes.

Gradually, as to be expected, the number lessened, but the custom was kept up during Mr. Brontë's stay. Mr. Mark Newsome, and Mr. Joseph

Newsome before him, told us of one enthusiastic admirer that walked over to Thornton three or four times on Sundays, solely to hear Mr. Brontë's utterances from the pulpit, and to exchange a few words of greeting. How often does an earnest and pious minister, leaving a sphere of labour where he has been some time, find that he is seemingly soon forgotten by the people for whom he had worked and prayed. Mr. Brontë seems to have had a different, a happier experience, so far as his young men were concerned.

The register books at Hartshead, if not as full of information respecting local events as those to be found in many parish churches, are of interest, and the present vicar is always most willing to show them to Brontë lovers. The oldest volume dates from 1612, and though the entries in it and subsequent books are of the briefest, will well repay inspection. Those of the mother church, we may state parenthetically, are of much greater value to the antiquary and the student of history. They go back to 1538, and form an unique record of the domestic history of the people of the district, and, as such, are of priceless value. The original orders for the provision of parish registers date from the year 1535, and were rendered necessary by the dissolution of the religious houses, and the consequent cessation of the registers. So far as Hartshead is concerned there is a serious hiatus in the chronicles—nearly one hundred years' registration of marriages, baptisms, and deaths being missing, and never likely to be supplied, unless from the archæpiscopal registers at York.

The first entry at Hartshead in which Mr. Brontë's name appears is dated March 31st, 1810, when he signed the record of baptisms. He was curate of Dewsbury church at that time, and had probably gone over to act for Mr. Lucas, the incumbent, who did not enjoy good health. Turning to the list of marriages, we note that the earliest by Mr. Brontë was in the following year—some seventeen months having elapsed since he wrote his name in the baptismal register—the following particulars being given: "Henry Taylor and Rachel Kay, both of this parish, were married in this church by Banns, this 25th August, 1811, by me, (signed) P. Brontë, minister.

This marriage was solemnized between us, the mark (X) of Henry Taylor, the mark (X) of Rachel Kay, in the presence of us, (signed) Luke Priestly, Geo. S. Sheard."

In the register book in use when Mr. Brontë became vicar there are fourteen marriages for 1811-12, and in the succeeding volume, wherein,

ROEHEAD, MIRFIELD, 1897.

under statutory regulations, certain printed forms had to be filled up, twenty-four.

The last wedding at which he officiated took place on the 15th of May, 1815, and the next record is one made six days later by the vicar from Thornton, with whom he had effected an exchange of livings, a bachelor, but who married shortly afterwards, and took as the pro-parsonage, Green House, Mirfield, a pleasant and comparatively spacious dwelling, attached to which was a good garden.

In this garden, when a school-girl at Roehead, Charlotte Brontë spent many happy hours, when on week-end visits to Mr. and Mrs. Atkinson, who were her god-parents. Mr. Atkinson remained in possession of the living at Hartshead till 1866, when owing to old age and bodily infirmity, he resigned. He died four years afterwards, namely, on the 28th of February, being then eighty-nine.

On asking Mr. King if he knew why Mr. Atkinson effected an exchange of livings with Mr. Brontë, he humorously replied, "He had a bird to catch, near Hartshead." Pressed for an explanation, he said the "bird" was Miss Walker, of Lascelles Hall, near Huddersfield, whom he afterwards married, and with whom he enjoyed long years of happiness.

CHAPTER XVI.

THE LUDDITES—MRS. BRONTË'S TIMIDITY—TROUBLOUS TIMES—THE ATTACK ON RAWFOLDS MILL—RIOTS AND MURDER—RIOTERS TRIED AND EXECUTED—MEN BURIED SECRETLY IN HARTSHEAD CHURCHYARD.

Whilst Mr. Brontë was incumbent of Hartshead, and for some time afterwards, a strong feeling was manifested amongst a large proportion of the operatives of the clothing districts of the West Riding against the further introduction of machinery, and the very serious disturbances known as the Luddite Riots took place. Trade was most depressed, wages low, employment scarce, and food, especially bread, dear. The hungry, ill-clad men and women became desperate, the former especially, and hence these disturbances. It has been said that Mrs. Brontë's strong desire to get into a quieter district than that on the borders of which she and her husband lived, was the reason why he effected an exchange with the incumbent of Thornton. Be that as it may, it is known that she was timid and uneasy, and though on good terms with the neighbours, was afraid of the violence in words, if not in deeds, of the frequently seen gangs of angry men, a few of whom were reputed to be from Nottingham, where many excesses had been committed, and others from south-east Lancashire. The assertion has been made, and doubtless correctly, that the lady's husband habitually carried pistols.

Those were troublous times in this as in other neighbourhoods. On the night of the 11th of April, 1812, occurred the desperate attack on Mr. Cartwright's mill at Rawfolds, only two miles from Hartshead, and which is described so vividly in *Shirley*. Beaten off, and with some bloodshed, the more violent of the Luddites determined on the assassination of some of the employers, and Mr. Wm. Horsfall, of Marsden, near Huddersfield, was killed, and several persons had narrow escapes.

The forces of the law at last prevailed. Sixty-six alleged rioters were arraigned at a Special Commission held at York Castle, and seventeen were executed, though three only participated in the murder of Mr. Horsfall. The last dread sentence was carried out on the 16th of January, 1813.

We are told by Mrs. Abm. Hirst, the aged lady already alluded to, and who has resided in the neighbourhood of Hartshead all her life, that Mr. Atkinson—in whose service she was for many years —had informed her that soon after the execution some of the bodies were brought secretly to High-town and interred in the dead of night, equally as secretly. Though the intention was to lay the deceased in consecrated ground in the district, if not in the immediate neighbourhood to which they belonged, no religious rite was used, beyond perhaps a brief prayer by one of the dead men's friends. Those were the days of the old constables, the roads were not patrolled at night as they now are, and there was not much likelihood of interruption, especially as the sympathies of the cottagers, if not of those of people of higher station in life, were with the relatives of those to whom the law had dealt out such terrible punishment. The burial party was therefore not disturbed either during the hasty digging of the graves, or in the actual interment. The place of sepulture is near the south-east corner of the churchyard, and contiguous to the highway.

That the inhabitants of the immediate neighbourhood knew what had occurred when they rose next morning may be taken for granted; but even strangers passing by could not help but see that something unusual had taken place in that corner of God's acre, in the soil lying roughly on the surface, and in the marks of many feet. There would be a sensation, and the parson would be hurriedly fetched; but perhaps

My dear Sir

I wish Farlam had given this ansr before. Mr Bailey would enquire at Bradford yesterday. Could you get Mr Bailey's success. If no success, if you write a note to Nevin, & can send it by Wilkinson to night to me, I will have it sent to Mirfield tomorrow. — I do not see what else can be done. I have some hopes by Mr Bailey.

Yours truly
H. Roberson

Healds Hall
15. Novr. 1839.

Wilkinson should not be detained he must be with me at $\frac{1}{4}$ past 5 precisely.

FAC-SIMILE OF A LETTER BY THE REVD. HAMMOND ROBERSON, M.A, knowing more than his flock gave him credit for, he wisely held his peace, and the dead lay as they do to-day, without a stone to mark the place of burial. Why should not a tomb be erected over the remains? All animosities long since vanished, and though who the deceased are is not known, a memorial slab would tell of the time as well as of the fact that beneath are the remains of our brothers.

Mr. F. Peel, in his interesting book, *The Rising of the Luddites*, gives an account of the recovery of the corpses of the executed and the bringing of them in carts through York, and there states that they were followed by thousands of people. The coffins contained the bodies of men from Huddersfield. There was no secrecy. On the contrary, a public demonstration doubtless continued to the time when lawful burial took place in the graveyards of the several towns or villages in the Huddersfield district to which they belonged. Why then should there be secret burial at Hartshead? In the contests that took place between the rioters and the representatives of the law at Rawfolds, and on the slopes of Liversedge, there were several persons shot and otherwise injured. Some of these, Mr. Peel says, were never heard of afterwards, to the great sorrow of their relatives. A few of the unfortunates—who had probably died in woods and copses, or in the cottages of sympathisers—it would be whose interment would have to be conducted secretly, for the safety of the living brought in contact with them. Hence the midnight funeral in Hartshead churchyard, at a spot contiguous to the quiet lane.

CHAPTER XVII.

MR. BRONTË AND HIS DAUGHTERS—FROM WHENCE DID THEY OBTAIN INSIGHT INTO WEST YORKSHIRE CHARACTER?—WHAT MRS. GASKELL AND DR. WRIGHT HAVE SAID—THE CHILDREN OF GENIUS FOR EVER LEARNING—THEIR FATHER AND ROBERSON AS CHARACTERS FOR "HELSTONE."

Mr. Brontë's experiences in this part of the West Riding were wide and varied, as has been seen, and they cannot but have greatly exercised his mind. He was quick of eye, as of brain, and had he chosen to have let his pen run in prose instead of in the poetry that only lives because of his illustrious daughters, he might have made some important contributions to literature. It has often been a subject of speculation with many readers how his daughters Charlotte, Emily, and Anne, especially the two first, gained a knowledge of the people among whom they lived, seeing that they were notoriously shy and reserved, and never mixed with them.

To them the West Riding character of the early part of the century—much more strongly marked than it is now, when the railways have done so much levelling up—was as an open book, and how rich is our literature in consequence. The girls went about timorously, certainly with shyness, but they were as resolute in their way as their father, and never failed to "gather the harvest of a quiet eye," and the comparative solitude in which they lived afforded them opportunities for study, and of the right kind.

How the moorlands amid which these frail geniuses lived entered into their lives and tinged their thoughts, others have told with graphic pens; but has sufficient consideration been given to the influence exercised upon their literary studies, consciously and unconsciously, by their strong old father? The man who at Dewsbury and Hartshead gave his mind to teaching the young, and, as we have seen, impressed them so much, would not neglect his own children. Pity that in Branwell his efforts had so little good result. "Canst thou minister to a mind diseased?" That of the erring son was indeed unhealthy.

Dr. Wright, in *The Brontës in Ireland*, a work that has been as abundantly praised as it has suffered vigorous criticism, furnishes much information that will enable students the better to understand this remarkable family. Dealing with the subject now under consideration he says: "Story-telling, as we shall see, was a hereditary gift in the Brontë family,

REVD. HAMMOND ROBERSON, M.A.

(From a miniature.)

and Patrick inherited it from his grandfather. Charlotte's friend, Miss Ellen Nussey, has often told me of the marvellous fascination with which the girls would hang on their father's lips as he depicted scene after scene of some tragic story in glowing words and with harrowing details. The breakfast would remain untouched till the story had passed the crisis, and sometimes the narration became so real and vivid and intense that the listeners begged the vicar to proceed no further. Sleepless nights succeeded story-telling evenings at the vicarage."

And Mrs. Gaskell, in her biography of Charlotte, tells us "The way in which Mr. Brontë made his children sympathise with him in his great interest in politics, must have done much to lift them above the chances of their minds being limited or tainted by petty local gossip." "Politics" meant with him something more than the great struggle on the Continent, which was to end with the downfall of Napoleon; the opening up of the nations to a renewal of friendly intercourse, and the relief of the people from part at least of the terrible strain they had had to bear. The word meant also the occurrences he had witnessed during his few years at Hartshead, and which to him and his household were of the greatest moment. Would not these form part of "the story-telling" in the early

Haworth days, when the minds of the children were most impressionable, and the "hereditary gift" in each so likely to be stimulated?

From whom, if not from her father, and the friends she made in Gomersal, Dewsbury Moor, and Mirfield, did Charlotte get the framework of the pictures she painted in *Shirley*, of the scenes at Rawfolds, and the portraits she etched in with so skilful a hand? Mr. Brontë must have witnessed much lawlessness, and have seen and taken note of this and that leader on either side. He was a man of keen powers of observation as well as of courage, had much knowledge of human nature, and he too would gather the harvest of a quiet eye, pouring the yield, years afterwards, into the minds of his daughters in the parlour of the Haworth parsonage, the son, too, taking part of the produce of the rich West Riding soil.

These children of genius were for ever learning, and for ever assimulating, and the tales of wilful, stubborn, headstrong men, the stories of love and tenderness as well as of brutual passions, were destined to be transmuted (by Charlotte and Emily most certainly) into the gold of their books, particularly in *Shirley*. It is said of Dickens that he wrote his father's character into "Micawber," and cannot it be asserted that we have Charlotte's parent over again in "Helstone," the other ex-curate of Dewsbury, Hammond Roberson, being made use of to complete the sketch of the man she wished to pourtray in the novel? Such a method of creation is common to the painter and the sculptor, and common also to numerous writers, to the very great advantage of all lovers of art and literature.

CHAPTER XVIII.

CHARLOTTE BRONTË.

THE CONNECTION OF CHARLOTTE WITH THE DEWSBURY DISTRICT —HER SCHOOL LIFE AT ROEHEAD—AS TEACHER AT DEWSBURY MOOR—HER THIRST FOR INFORMATION—AN OLD CUSTOM AT DEWSBURY EXCITES HER ATTENTION.

Though the connection with the Dewsbury district of the author of *Jane Eyre*—and hereabouts at all events—of her still more popular novel, *Shirley*, is comparatively slight, a chapter may fittingly be devoted to the distinguished lady. Her first known visit to this neighbourhood was when she became a pupil of Miss Wooler, at Roehead. The expense of her education was borne by her god-parents, the Revd. Thos. Atkinson, vicar of Hartshead, and Mrs. Atkinson, his wife, and she spent with them several week-ends at the pro-parsonage, Green House, Mirfield, attached to which is a large garden. One of the servants,—now, and for many years past—Mrs. Abm. Hirst, of Roberttown, already named, was always sent for Charlotte, and took her back to school on Monday mornings, and she recollects her as an exceedingly shy, if not a timid and shrinking girl, observant of the beauties of nature in the lovely neighbourhood; spare of speech and nice in manners, though somewhat awkward, and evidently observant. The Atkinsons were very fond of the lassie, who, however, never seemed so much at ease as when alone in the garden.

Charlotte was a visitor also at a later period, when her position at Miss Wooler's academy had become that of teacher. It is not recollected that Emily either accompanied her sister to the Atkinsons during the three short months she was at Roehead, or that Anne went to see them. In her womanhood Charlotte did not call at Green House—certainly not after she became an authoress—for Mrs. Atkinson caused it to be made known to her that she was much displeased at the way in which she had written of the clergy. Besides, the good, but narrow-minded lady, "did not approve of women writing novels," and *Jane Eyre* seems to have shocked her, as also did *Shirley*, with its three curates, so ably and unsparingly caricatured.

In 1836, Miss Wooler gave up her school at Roehead, and took Healds House, Dewsbury Moor, formerly the residence of the Revd. Hammond Roberson. One of our informants of twelve years ago, said he well remembered the flitting, and how it was conducted, and that it gave much amusement to himself and other boys, as well as to the scholars, most of whom, however, had gone to their respective homes till Miss Wooler had prepared the new school for them.

At Dewsbury Moor, as had been the custom at the Mirfield establishment, the girls were taken out daily, weather permitting, and Miss Brontë was in charge. She also accompanied them, on Sundays, to St. John's Church, Dewsbury Moor, with Miss Wooler. The vicar then was the Rev. John Payne, M.A., formerly of Bentley, near Doncaster, who himself had a boarding school of considerably more than local celebrity.

It is worthy of mention that one of his pupils was a boy from near Keighley, John Brigg, now a member of Parliament. This gentleman, who resides at Kildwick Hall, was a leading promoter of the establishment of the Brontë Society, and of the formation of the interesting museum at Haworth. He was the first chairman of the council of the Society, and continues to take an active interest in all that relates to the Brontës and Brontë literature.

Many have supposed that while Charlotte was engaged in the, to her, hateful occupation of teaching at Dewsbury Moor, she was not visited by any of her relatives. Her father came over at least on one occasion, and he was certainly seen coming from a direction that leads to the conclusion that he had been to Healds House.

The person who saw him was the late Mrs. Thos. Stocks, the wife of a farmer who formerly resided at Greenhead farm, if she did not actually live there at the time. Mrs. Stocks worshipped at Dewsbury Parish Church when Mr. Brontë was curate there, and she recognised him instantly, and told the members of her household. When observed by her he was walking along Primrose Lane, an occupation road passing through the farm, and leading from Dewsbury Moor to Mirfield. It was a lane not open to the public, but affording, as it did, a short cut to the latter township, or to Hartshead, if he was journeying to the scene of his former labours, Mr. Brontë had no hesitation seemingly of making use of it.

Charlotte was often seen, of course, and some of those who noticed her when in charge of Miss Wooler's young ladies, are Mrs. W. Steele and Mrs. G. Tolson, of Dewsbury, daughters of Mrs. Stocks, and the Misses Smith, of Dewsbury Moor. The oldest of the two latter, who gave us some interesting information about three years ago, died recently.

Her brother Robert, who predeceased her, saw

much more of the future great novelist than either of his sisters. He was often employed to drive her to Gomersal and to Birstall, when she visited her friends the Taylors and Miss Nussey, and was fond of chatting about her to old friends. "Miss Brontë" he said "would never enter into conversation with me, further than asking questions as we drove along. She was inquisitive, though, about the people that lived in the district, and would point to first one place and then another and enquire who lived there; and the next time we went, or when I was fetching her back next day, or at night, she would ask what sort of people they were."

Mr. Smith told us he had the impression that she must have put down on paper what he told her, and that he was confirmed in this, because, on subsequent journeys, she questioned him again about ladies and gentlemen he had named in his replies. He said, in one of the interviews we had with him, that he once or twice mustered courage to ask Miss Brontë a question, and that she answered him in the briefest way, and shewed by her manner that she desired he would not presume, but keep his place--that of driver of the vehicle hired from his father, a farmer. To use his words, "She freezed up, if *I* wanted to know anything." Her dress, he stated, was always plain, and though exquisitely neat, gave him the impression that the wearer was a person of straitened means.

Asked if he thought she took most pleasure in going to Birstall or Gomersal Mr. Smith answered "Birstall, judging by the regret she showed in parting from her friend." This lady, venerable in years, is still active in mind and body, and all Brontë-lovers are grateful to her for what she has done in permitting the publication of letters

DEWSBURY PARISH CHURCH, WHEN CHARLOTTE BRONTË WAS A WORSHIPPER.

addressed to her by Charlotte, and in furnishing particulars to this and that writer about the gifted being, as school companion, bosom friend, authoress, and wife.

Charlotte, on Sunday evenings, except in mid-winter, often attended service at Dewsbury Old Church, the scene of her father's ministrations a quarter of a century or more before, and Robert Smith attended as her guard and protector, in case protection was required; but the people, if rough in manner, were kindly, and well-meaning, and she was never interfered with on her way homewards or to church, long though the walk was.

Occasionally, she came into Dewsbury for shopping purposes, and the son of an old tradesman has told us that his father did business with Miss Wooler when she kept the school at Healds House. Some, at least of the teachers, did also, and when *Jane Eyre* came out, and the fame of the author was established, and her name become known, his father told a knot of friends who were discussing the novelist and her work, that he believed he could find an old ledger that had been packed away, in which her name appeared. A search was made for it, and being discovered, it was found to contain the entry, "Miss Brontë, at Healds House."

We have stated—what all the world knows—that she was observant, and was also a close questioner. Had the demure damsel been of the other sex, and a barrister, cross-examination would have been her *forte*. She certainly had an enquiring mind. Let us see how she applied it to a street scene in Dewsbury. For generations it has been a custom for a sometimes not small crowd to assemble near the gates of the Parish church, on a Sunday evening, to witness the dispersal of the congregation, and to greet friends and sweethearts coming out of the gate of the graveyard, in Church street. There is a convenient bend. The stocks stood there in ancient times, and, it may be, the spot was a resort for those who failed to find much to interest them in other streets of the town.

Miss Brontë appeared to be struck with the concourse of waiting folk, and doubtless thought they would have been much better inside the church; and one evening, when returning to Healds House, after service, she called the attentive Robert to her side, and asked if he knew why non-worshippers assembled in such numbers near the church gates when the congregation was dispersing. He told her he did not, that "folk were always there," and that he would enquire. He did so, and made a point of speaking to old people, for he "wanted to please Miss Brontë."

On the following Sunday evening, when they were passing along a field-path near where now runs Healds road—a thoroughfare leading from Halifax road to Staincliffe road—she called the youth up, and asked, "Did you enquire why a crowd assembles at the Old Church gates on Sunday nights?" He replied that he had spoken to several aged folk, who could only tell him it was an old custom to go there, and had been kept up all their lives. As to its origin, he could learn nothing, he told her.

The custom, such as it is, has not fallen into disuetude.

CHAPTER XIX.

LAST SCENE OF ALL.

A few lines more and we part both with Charlotte and her venerable father. It is the early morn on the 31st of March, 1855, and there is deep gloom in the Haworth parsonage. The bell in the tower of the church begun to toll, and conveyed the sad news to the people of the valley and hill that the gifted woman was no more; the brave heart had ceased to beat, and the hands could clasp no more those of the loving husband and father standing by the bedside; and the younger man was bathed in tears of unavailing grief. But the figure at his side! What of the man from whom fell disease had now torn all his family, Charlotte being the last to go? His tall and venerable form was as upright as the long years permitted. His face was calm, his words soothing, yet strong, conveying consolation to the bereaved young man, sunk where lay the corpse of his wife. An hour or so passed, the aged father, self reliant, though inwardly torn with grief, giving the support the other needed so much, and bringing at length outward composure if not an assuagement of sorrow.

Then Mr. Brontë left for his own chamber to get much needed rest, and in a few minutes a woman assisting the household in that time of direst trouble, entered, not knowing he was there, to perform some duty. She had seen him so strong—stern as she thought — yet sympathetic, when consoling the afflicted husband of her who had gone, and wondered; but now she found the real man. He was on his knees in the attitude of prayer, and in an agony of grief, bemoaning the loss of her whom he pitifully called, "My dear Charlotte! My dear Charlotte!"

Yes, the woman had wondered at his calmness when death came; his coldness she thought it; and she saw that, while strong for others, he was now as a little child, and resting on his Father.

Retiring with a heart full of sympathy, she said to herself, "I understand Mr. Brontë better now; I never understood him before."

Yes, times of sorrow try us all, and fortunate are we if tribulation leads to a better understanding of each other.

FINIS.

APPENDICES

PORTRAIT OF THE REV. P. BRONTE IN 1809, in which year he came to Dewsbury.

In the Press, and will shortly be Published.

Large Crown 8vo. Price to Subscribers 5s., Post Free.

"The Father of the Brontes,"

His Life and Work in Dewsbury and Hartshead,

With a Chapter on "Currer Bell,"

AND A *FAC SIMILE* OF AN HITHERTO UNPUBLISHED LETTER.

BY W. W. YATES,

(Fellow of the Institute of Journalists.)

In this Book will be found much interesting information hitherto unknown to the public, obtained by long and careful investigation.

[P.T.O.]

ADVERTISEMENT FOR ORIGINAL BOOK

APPENDIX I

Joseph Horsfall Turner was born in Brighouse and became a schoolmaster. He moved to Bradford to be a headmaster. A well-known historian and antiquarian, he wrote numerous books including *Haworth Past and Present*; *Brontëana* and many other books and articles.

He went to London to train as a teacher and on leaving became a teacher for 2 years at the International British School in Lancaster. He then came back to Brighouse to teach at a private school. He was very involved in the Brighouse Congregational Church and its pupils. In his day Horsfall Turner was regarded as one of the most diligent record researchers in the West Riding. Before the start of the Brontë Society together with some other founder members, such as Mr Butler Wood, Bradford librarian and William Scruton, solicitors clerk and writer, they were members of the Bradford Antiquarian Society. They tried to save the old St. Michaels Church, Haworth in 1879 where Rev Patrick Brontë was incumbent and the Brontë family, except Anne, were buried in the church crypt. They saved the church tower, although a new church was built.

In 1861 Horsfall Turner when he was 16 years old walked from Brighouse to Haworth to visit the grave of Rev Patrick Brontë. He also visited the niece of Rev Patrick Brontë, Rose Ann Heslip, whose mother Sarah was one of Rev Patrick Brontë's sisters. Rose Heslip came to live in Salthorn, Oakenshaw near Cleckheaton. She had read about what Dr William

LEFT TO RIGHT: ELIZABETH ANN, HUGH BINGHAM, MARY JANE, ROSE ANN HESLIP *(SEATED)*

Wright had written about her family in Ireland from an article in a Bradford newspaper. She was not happy with the article and asserted much was untrue so she sent her son-in-law, Hugh Bingham, to London to speak to Dr Wright who came back to visit her. Horsfall Turner attended Rose Ann Heslip's funeral at Whitechapel Church, Cleckheaton on the 15th March 1915 with other members of the Brontë Society. Horsfall Turner himself died several weeks later on the 2nd May 1915 aged 71 years leaving a widow and the surviving members of his ten children. He visited Charlotte Brontë's husband, Rev Arthur Bell Nicholls, at his home in Banagher, Ireland. Arthur's second wife, Mary Bell Nicholls, sold Horsfall Turner a lock of Charlotte Brontë's hair, several Brontë letters, a sampler worked by Charlotte, a miniature portrait of Mrs Brontë, and a watercolour picture of Anne Brontë painted by Charlotte Brontë. He was also given as a souvenir a medallion of Patrick Branwell Brontë, the work of J B Leyland the Halifax sculptor, which is in the Brontë Parsonage. He visited Brontë descendants in Northern Ireland and wrote accounts of his interviews with them in his book *Brontëana*.

Horsfall Turner corresponded with and visited Ellen Nussey who was a school friend of Charlotte Brontë. Ellen Nussey also visited Horsfall Turner's home in Idle, Bradford. J Horsfall Turner was a Liberal councillor in Idle, Bradford and also a local Justice of the Peace.

APPENDIX II

Frank Peel was born in Great Horton, Bradford in 1831 the son of Edward Peel a small worsted manufacturer. He did not follow his father's profession but instead was apprenticed to a linen draper, Fred Hinings of Bradford. Frank married into the Hinings family and wed Harriet Emma Hinings his employer's youngest sister. He went into partnership with his brother-in-law in a newly established firm of linen drapers, Hinings and Peel, in Market Street, Heckmondwike.

After a few years Frank dissolved the partnership but was very enterprising and continued his linen drapery business and other enterprises. He developed a strong liking for literary pursuits and commenced to write on a variety of subjects as a local correspondent for the Heckmondwike Reporter. His drapers shop was in a strategic position in town so customers would bring stories, information and memories so that the quick mind of Frank would note this information as potential material for what was to be his real life's work.

In 1892 Charles F Forman brought out Frank Peel's book *The Poems of Spen Valley* which included three of Frank Peel's own poems and a short biography. In 1896 Frank retired from his drapers shop that he had owned for 30 years and moved not far from the town centre to Union Road, Heckmondwike with his family. He became editor and co-proprietor with Albert Senior of the *Heckmondwike Herald*. The newspaper flourished and had five local editions which came out on a Thursday, namely *Heckmondwike*, *Mirfield*, *Birstall* and

Thornhill Heralds and *Spen Valley Times*. It was in these newspapers and the *Cleckheaton Guardian* that the material found in his books first appeared as newspaper articles.

Frank Peel was the author of the books *Spen Valley Past and Present*'; *The Rising of the Luddites* and *Nonconformity in the Spen Valley* and many other publications. He was an ardent supporter of religious work in the town and became a member of the George Street Congregational Church. He later severed his connection with that church and joined the Wesleyan Church and was actively engaged in the Sunday School for 25 years. In later years he returned to the Congregational Church. At his funeral young men from both churches were pole-bearers of his coffin. His efforts to stop the sale of intoxicating drinks gained him the gratitude of many in the community.

Mr Peel figured prominently as an antiquarian being one of the most active members in the local Society. The Antiquarian Society of Scotland conferred on him fellowship of the Society to make him an FSAS. He was honorary secretary of the Heckmondwike Antiquarian Society. He was secretary for many years to the Trademans' Association and the Heckmondwike Chamber of Commerce. In politics Frank Peel was a Radical and served a three year term on the Heckmondwike Local Board after being elected by a large majority.

Frank Peel was a founder member of the Brontë Society and served on the Brontë Society Council. He interviewed Rev Patrick Brontë's niece, Rose Ann Heslip (her mother Sarah being one of Patrick Brontë's sisters) who came to live in Oakenshaw on the Cleckheaton-Bradford boundary. Frank Peel died at his home in Heckmondwike on 10th April 1900 leaving a widow, two sons and three daughters. He was buried in Heckmondwike cemetery and Mr J J Stead; Joseph Horsfall Turner and Mr W W Yates attended the funeral from the Brontë Society.

APPENDIX III

JOHN JAMES STEAD was born in 1841 the eldest son of Thomas Stead, who owned and managed Messr Abraham Stead & Sons, Drysalter and Dyewood Cutters of Valley Mills, Heckmondwike. Thomas Stead was a local preacher at the Primitive Methodist Church and his wife was a United Methodist. John James Stead followed in his mother's footsteps into the church. In childhood he manifested an interest in religion unusual for a lad of his age. He gave lifelong service to the church from Sunday School teaching to the Office of Treasurer to the Church Trustees. His connections with the Methodist church extended over 70 years. He wrote about the history of the United Methodist Church in Heckmondwike and had it published with the assistance of friends.

Mr Stead was one of the founder members of the Brontë Society and served on the Brontë Council. He possessed a wealth of information and books that had to do with the history of the Brontë family. He was of great service to such famous literary men of his time as Clement Shorter, Robertson Nicholl, Helliwell Sutcliffe, Frank Peel, Claude Meeker and Harry Speight, a relative to the Stead family through marriage. These gentlemen had expressed personal thanks to Mr Stead for his ready and kind co-operation.

Photography was one of his great hobbies and through it he preserved for future generations pictures of old buildings and landmarks in West Yorkshire, some of these long since demolished. The Spen Valley Literary and Scientific Society had in him an earnest, consistent supporter and he was happy to assist many other societies. Amongst these he was a member of Old Heckmondwike Naturalist and Antiquarian Society, Yorkshire Archaeological Society, Yorkshire Naturalist Union and Dialect Society.

John Stead retired some 20 years before his death from the family firm. He was a member of Heckmondwike School Board. For 27 years he was a director of Heckmondwike & Liversedge Gas Company and for 15 years held the position of chairman. He died aged 78 at his home in Heckmondwike on 23rd October 1919 leaving a widow, daughter and a son, who was a local architect in the town. Many people attended his funeral and he was buried in Heckmondwike cemetery.

APPENDIX IV

Dr J A Erskine Stuart was born in Scotland and studied to be a doctor. He became a ship's doctor. He then came to Yorkshire and had a doctor's practice and surgery in Heckmondwike and Batley. He became Public Officer of Health in Batley.

He wrote many papers on medicine and surgery. He was interested in literature and walking. He wrote the *Bronte Country* and the *Literary Shrines of Yorkshire.* He visited Ellen Nussey and became a personal friend and advisor to her. They exchanged correspondence and the letters are in the Brontë Parsonage Museum library. Dr Stuart in later retirement came to live in Mirfield and died at his home Woodlands, Hopton, Mirfield in December 1927 aged 73 leaving a wife, two daughters and a son in California. He was on the Brontë Council and gave one of the first talks to the Society at its first Annual General Meeting in Dewsbury 1894.

Claude Meeker held the post of United States consul to Bradford, West Yorkshire and was long connected with American journalism. He commenced his press career at 18 and by age 21 was editor and co-proprietor of a successful weekly journal devoted to literature, art and drama. He was a regular contributor of vigorous political and social articles to the *New York World, Boston Globe, Washington Post, Chicago Tribune, St. Louis Republic* and other influential newspapers in the United States. It is however with the Cincinnati journals that he has been most connected, being at different times on the staff of the Cincinnati News-Journal, Enquirer, Post and the Times Star. Coming from the pen of such an experienced journalist as Mr Meeker, he wrote the small book Haworth, Home of the Brontës which was included in the Brontë Society Transactions in 1895. Mr Meeker's description of his visit to Haworth brings home to us the fact that the American people have been amongst the first to recognise and appreciate the writings of the Brontës. It is shown not only in admiration of the Brontë writings but in the frequent pilgrimages to Haworth by American visitors. A beautiful memorial window has been donated by an American gentleman, George W Childs of Philadelphia, widely known for his philanthropic work, to St. Michaels Church, Haworth in memory of Charlotte Brontë.

In the *Times Star* appeared an illustrated article on 'Haworth, Home of the Brontes' from the pen of Claude Meeker. It will have been read with keen interest by all lovers of literature who have been entranced by the pages of *Jane Eyre*, *The Professor*, *Wuthering Heights*, *The Tenant of Wildfell Hall*, *Agnes Grey*, *Villette*, *Shirley* and other works of the immortal sisters. The value of Mr Meeker's work, which was written for the *Times Star,* is its geographical and historic accuracy as well as its rich literacy flavour. Mr Meeker also thanked Mr J J Stead of Heckmondwike for permission to reproduce his illustrations.